THE MOTOR CAMPING BOOK

A MANUAL ON EARLY CAR CAMPING AND CLASSIC RECREATIONAL TRAVEL

BY **ELON JESSUP**

FIRST PUBLISHED IN 1921

LEGACY EDITION
THE LIBRARY OF AMERICAN OUTDOORS CLASSICS

FEATURING
REMASTERED CLASSIC WORKS OF THE HIGHEST QUALITY
FROM **THE TIMELESS MASTERS AND TEACHERS**
OF CAMPING, OUTDOORS SKILLS, WOODCRAFT,
AND TRADITIONAL HANDCRAFTS

Doublebit Press

New content, introduction, and annotations
Copyright © 2021 by Doublebit Press. All rights reserved.
www.doublebitpress.com | Cherry, IL, USA

First published in 1921 by Elon Jessup.

Doublebit Press Legacy Edition ISBNs
Hardcover: 978-1-64389-188-0
Paperback: 978-1-64389-189-7

WARNING: Some of the material in this book may be outdated by modern safety standards. This antique text may contain outdated and unsafe recreational activities, projects, or mechanical, electrical, chemical, or medical practices. Any use of this book for purposes other than historic study may result in unsafe and hazardous conditions and individuals act at their own risk and are responsible for their own safety. Doublebit Press, its authors, or its agents assume no liability for any injury, harm, or damages to persons or property arising either directly or indirectly from any content contained in this text or the activities performed by readers. Remember to be safe with any activity or work you do and use good judgement by following proper health and safety protocols. In addition, because this book was from a past time and is presented in an unabridged form, the contents may be culturally or racially insensitive. Such content does not represent the opinions or positions of the publisher and are presented for historical posterity and accuracy to the original text.

DISCLAIMER: Doublebit Press has not tested or analyzed the methods, materials, and practices appearing in this public domain text and provides no warranty to the accuracy and reliability of the content. This text is provided only as a reprinted facsimile from the unedited public domain original as first published and authored. This text is published for historical study and personal literary enrichment purposes only and should only be used for such. The publisher assumes no liability for any injury, harm, or damages to persons or property arising either directly or indirectly from any information contained in this public domain book or activities performed by readers.

INTRODUCTION
To The Doublebit Press Legacy Edition

The old experts of the woods and mountains taught timeless principles and skills for decades. Through their books, the old experts offered rich descriptions of the outdoor world and encouraged learning through personal experiences in nature. Over the last 125 years, camping, outdoors recreation, and woods activities have substantially changed. Many things have gotten simpler as gear has improved, and life outside or on the trail now brings with it many of the same comforts enjoyed in town. In addition, some activities of the olden days are now no longer in vogue, or are even outright considered inappropriate or illegal, such as high-impact camping practices like chopping down live trees. However, despite many of the positive changes in outdoors methods that have occurred over the years, *there are many other skills and much knowledge that have been forgotten* from the golden era of American outdoors recreation.

By publishing the Library of American Outdoors Classics, it is our goal at Doublebit Press to do what we can to preserve and share the works from forgotten teachers that form the cornerstone of the history of the American outdoors. Through remastered reprint editions of timeless classics of outdoor recreation, perhaps we can regain some of this lost knowledge for future generations.

Because there were fewer options for finding outdoors gear in the early 1900's, experts in *"woodcraft"* skills (not to be confused with today's use of the word to mean woodworking or making things of wood) had to have a deep knowledge of the basic building blocks of outdoor living. This involved not only surviving in the outdoors, but to also have a comfortable and enjoyable time. As Nessmuk puts it in his book *Woodcraft,* "We do not go to the woods to rough it; we go to smooth it — we get it rough enough in town. But let us live the simple, natural life in the woods, and leave all frills behind." Nessmuk did not advocate for folks to go outside and have a terrible time. That would be contrary to the whole point of getting outside. Instead, he advocated for a "simpler" life by leaving some of the creature comforts of the city behind, but also entering the outdoors in a smart and practiced way that made the experience a much more satisfying vacation from home. The goal is to be comfortable so you can focus on having a good time outside and take in everything exposure to nature can offer. However, to be comfortable, one has to know the ins and outs of camping and outdoors life. Despite all the advances in campcraft and outdoors recreation, the old masters of the woods would all likely argue that this will only come from practicing the basics.

Because there was no market yet for specialty outdoors recreational gear (and thus, few outfitters), most outdoors gear came from military surplus piles or was custom made. As such, the old masters of woodcraft often made their own gear suited to their tastes. Through much experience in the woods and field, the great outdoors experts had to know why things worked the way they did by understanding the great web of cause and effect in nature. They had to learn from experience why certain gear worked better in different conditions or know how to solve problems off-the-cuff when things got hairy. They used the basic blocks of camping and outdoors knowledge to fine-tune their gear. They gained experience whenever they could and tried things different ways so they could gain mastery over the fundamentals and see challenges from many angles.

Today, much of the outdoor experience has been greatly simplified by neatly arranged campsites at public campgrounds and gear that has been meticulously improved and tested in both the lab and the field. Many modern conveniences are only a brief trek away, with many parks, campgrounds, and even forests having easy-access roads, convenience stores, and even cell phone signal. In some ways, it is much easier to camp and go outdoors today, and that is a good thing! We should not be miserable when we go outside — lovers of the outdoors know the essential restorative capability that the woods can have on the body, mind, and soul. Although things have gotten easier on us in the 21st Century when it comes to the outdoors, it certainly does not mean that we should forget the foundations of outdoors lore, though. All modern camping skills, outdoors equipment, and cool gizmos that make our lives easier are all founded on principles of the outdoors that the old masters knew well and taught to those who would listen.

Every woods master had their own curriculum or thought some things were more important than others. This includes the present author — certain things appear in this book that other masters leave out of theirs. The old masters also taught common things in slightly different ways or did things differently than others. That's what makes each of the experts different and worth reading. There's no universal way of doing something, especially now. Learning to go about something differently helps with mastery or learn a new skill altogether. Again, to use the metaphor from the above paragraphs, outdoors skills mastery consists of learning the basic building blocks of outdoors living, woods and nature lore, and the art of packing properly for trips. Each master goes about describing these building blocks differently or shows a different aspect of them.

Therefore, we have decided to publish this Legacy Edition in our Library of American Outdoors Classics series. This book is an important contribution to the early American recreational outdoors literature and has important historical and collector value toward preserving the American outdoors tradition. The knowledge it holds is an invaluable reference for practicing skills and hand craft methods. Its chapters thoroughly discuss some of the essential building blocks of knowledge that are fundamental but may have been forgotten as equipment gets fancier and technology gets smarter. In short, this book was chosen for Legacy Edition printing because much of the basic skills and knowledge it contains has been forgotten or put to the wayside in trade for more modern conveniences and methods.

Although the editors at Doublebit Press are thrilled to have comfortable experiences in the woods and love our high-tech and light-weight equipment, we are also realizing that the basic skills taught by the old masters are more essential than ever as our culture becomes more and more hooked on digital stuff. We don't want to risk forgetting the important steps, skills, or building blocks involved with thriving in the outdoors. The Legacy Edition series represents the essential contributions to the American outdoors tradition by the great experts of outdoors life and traditional hand crafting.

With technology playing a major role in everyday life, sometimes we need to take a step back in time to find those basic building blocks used for gaining mastery – the things that we have luckily not completely lost and has been recorded in books over the last two centuries. These skills aren't forgotten, they've just been shelved. *It's time to unshelve them once again and reclaim the lost knowledge of self-sufficiency.*

Based on this commitment to preserving our outdoors and handcraft heritage, we have taken great pride in publishing this book as a complete original work. We hope it is worthy of both study and collection by outdoors folk in the modern era of outdoors and traditional skills life.

Unlike many other photocopy reproductions of classic books that are common on the market, this Legacy Edition does not simply place poor photography of old texts on our pages and use error-prone optical scanning or computer-generated text. We want our work to speak for itself, and reflect the quality demanded by our customers who spend their hard-earned money. With this in mind, each Legacy Edition book that has been chosen for publication is carefully remastered from original print books, *with the Doublebit Legacy Edition printed and laid out in the exact way that it was presented at its original publication.* We provide a beautiful, memorable experience that is as true to the original text as best as possible, but with the aid of modern technology to make as beautiful a reading experience as possible for books that are typically over a century old.

Because of its age and because it is presented in its original form, the book may contain misspellings, inking errors, and other print blemishes that were common for the age. However, these are exactly the things that we feel give the book its character, which we preserved in this Legacy Edition. During digitization, we ensured that each illustration in the text was clean and sharp with the least amount of loss from being copied and digitized as possible. Full-page plate illustrations are presented as they were found, often including the extra blank page that was often behind a plate. For the covers, we use the original cover design to give the book its original feel. We are sure you'll appreciate the fine touches and attention to detail that your Legacy Edition has to offer.

For outdoors enthusiasts who demand the best from their equipment, this Doublebit Press Legacy Edition reprint was made with you in mind. Both important and minor details have equally both been accounted for by our publishing staff, down to the cover, font, layout, and images. It is the goal of Doublebit Legacy Edition series to preserve outdoors heritage, but also be cherished as collectible pieces, worthy of collection in any outdoorsperson's library and that can be passed to future generations.

Every book selected to be in this series offers unique views and instruction on important skills, advice, tips, tidbits, anecdotes, stories, and experiences that will enrich the repertoire of any person who enjoys escaping the city and finding their way to the trails of the wilds. To learn the most basic building blocks of outdoors life leads to mastery of all its aspects.

Studying This Book

The pages within this book present an overwhelming amount of information, facts, and directions to memorize that are often outdated and at the least, out of practice by modern standards. That doesn't mean that these pages have nothing to teach! It's just going to likely be new stuff for many readers.

Our one suggestion is *don't try to memorize everything,* especially when you're thumbing through the book or even reading it cover-to-cover. Writings from the late 1800's to early 1900's can be dense and out of style for someone not used to reading these types of books. Instead, gain some basic familiarity with each topic by thumbing through the pages, looking at the illustrations, and seeing the section headers. Then, choose a few topics or skills for deeper study.

Before camping or other outdoors trips can even begin, some planning and reflection is useful, which may be best done in town before you go out to the field. First, it might be helpful to read through the book with plans in mind. The book can provide useful material for close study and reflection when in town before you head out to the field to practice.

Secondly, once you've come up with a practice plan, you will of course want to start doing tasks and skills in the field. Doublebit Legacy books and the Library of American Outdoors Classics represents many field skills to master that have long sense been out of practice, but hopefully not forgotten! These include making and trying different kinds of tents or shelters, cooking (including any fish and game caught by you in the field), making many types of fires, setting up camp to suit your personal needs, beating the bugs and elements, understanding the terrain and weather, making furniture, brushing up on your nature lore, emergency survival, and testing your personal outfit and tools.

Any of the old tutors of woodcraft will tell you in their classic books that you can only truly learn how to go camping and do woodcraft by *actually doing it*. Home study indeed does you well by using the many guidebooks that have been published over the previous 125 years. However, hundreds more lessons will become immediately available to you the moment you start with some of the old-style tasks. This old style of outdoorsing is indeed outdated in many ways, but the approach still has much to teach modern campers who have become accustomed to carved out campsites, cabin and RV camping, and high-tech equipment.

Before the days of outfitters, outdoors adventurers made their gear, which was tailored to their individual needs. Many experiments were done in the field to tweak their gear to get that ever-changing point of "perfect." Aside from experiencing wonderful lessons in history, getting outside and doing some of the activities this book will give you an appreciation for modern advances in outdoors and handcraft method and tools of the trade, as well as a deeper understanding of the foundations of outdoors and hand-craft life in the event that your gear fails you or you otherwise find yourself in situations where knowing the principles will get you unstuck fast.

If we were to tally up each of the individual tips in the Doublebit Library of American Outdoors Classics, they would easily number in the thousands. The old masters represent centuries of previous knowledge that have been all but lost to 21st Century, technology-driven folks. To this point, although experience and *actually doing stuff* are the best forms of learning, taking a mindful approach to study of these works also benefit your development as a competent outdoorsperson and handcrafter.

You may also find it invaluable to take these volumes with you on your camping or other outdoors trips. In addition to having reading material on a variety of topics in the field for down time, you'll also find a thousand things to try in these pages if you're bored. Although skills may be best studied when in the field through experience and reflection, you may also study woods skills at home as well. Gaining familiarity through reading, videos, and other media are a great start toward building your ability toward gaining mastery in the field.

So, without blabbering on further, we hope you enjoy your Doublebit Legacy Edition. May your trails be clear and your experiences be memorable!

- The Doublebit Press Editors

The Motor Camping Book

By

Elon Jessup

Associate Editor of "Outing," Author of "Intimate Golf Talks"

With 100 Illustrations

G. P. Putnam's Sons
New York and London
The Knickerbocker Press
1921

Copyright, 1921
BY
G. P. PUTNAM'S SONS

TO YOU

AND ALL OTHERS WHO KNOW OR WILL KNOW THE FUN OF MOTOR CAMPING, THIS BOOK IS DEDICATED. MAY IT SERVE AS A SIGNPOST TO HEALTH AND HAPPINESS.

CONTENTS

CHAPTER	PAGE
I.—Why we Motor-Camp	1
II.—The Importance of Right Equipment	9
III.—The Car and the Pack	18
IV.—Water Containers	35
V.—The Cooking Kit	47
VI.—The Cooking Fire	58
VII.—Food Boxes	77
VIII.—The Night's Sleep	89
IX.—Sleeping in the Car	103
X.—Combination Beds and Tents	110
XI.—Motor Camping Tents	124
XII.—The Camping Trailer	137
XIII.—Camp Furnishings	149
XIV.—Getting out of Trouble	164

CONTENTS

CHAPTER		PAGE
XV.—Motor Camping Trails		178
XVI.—Where to Go Motor Camping		189
XVII.—The Law and the Motorist		202
Index		217

ILLUSTRATIONS

A Western Camping Ground for Touring Motorists	*Frontispiece*
A Comfortable Long-Time Camp	12
Running-Board Bed and Tent	16
Suit-Case Cover Diagram	25
Car Baby Crib	30
Folding Luggage Carrier	32
Bracket Luggage Carrier	33
Bar Luggage Carrier	34
The Canvas Water Bag	41
Running-Board Canteens	44
Wash Basin, Stand, and Bath Tubs	44
Folding Canvas Bucket	45
Six-Person Aluminum Cooking Outfit	53
Vacuum Bottle, Fry Pan, Salt Shaker, and Food Container	56
Solidified Alcohol Stove	60
Kerosene Stove	62
A Stove which Burns either Gasoline or Kerosene	64
Detailed Drawing of a Two-Burner Gasoline Stove	67

ILLUSTRATIONS

	PAGE
Camp Grates	71
Camp Grate with Charcoal Fire	72
Camp Grate with Wind Shield	73
The Oven Section of a Folding Stove	74
Combination Bed and Tent; a Folding Camp Stove	74
Sheet Metal Running-Board Food Box	78
Running-Board Box and a Refrigerator Basket	82
The Whimsical, Hungry Porcupine	86
Sleeping Bag with Canvas Cover	92
Laying a Bough Bed	94
Types of Folding Cots	96
The Double Cot and Tent Framework	98
Outdoor Rug; Kapok Mattress; Air Mattress	100
Suspended Canvas Car Bed	106
Car Cots	108
Bed with Canvas Shelter	112
The Double Cot with Canvas Overhead	114
A Unique One-Legged Bed with Tent	115
Operations of Folding a Running-Board Outfit	119
Running-Board Outfit both Packed and Set Up	120
Steel Bed and Tent	122

ILLUSTRATIONS

	PAGE
Steel Bed with Tent Variations	122
A Combination Outfit Packed on the Running Board	123
A Single Lean-To Tent; a Camping Trailer	126
Car Slip-On Covers	127
Single and Double Tents	128
Tent with Back Guys Tied to Car	129
Wall and Marquee Tents	130
Wedge Tent Attached to Car	132
Lean-To Tents Combined; a Car Bed	134
Two Tents Attached to Car	134
Off to the Woods with a Camping Trailer	138
Camping Trailer Packed and Set up	142
The Motor Bungalo	146
Backing around Corners with a Trailer	148
Bed Doing Table Service	151
A Camper Builds his own Furniture	152
Two Types of Folding Tables	154
An Adjustable Table	155
Folding Camp Chair	156
Camp Wall Pocket	157
Folding Candle Lantern	159
A Pull-Out Device	168

ILLUSTRATIONS

	PAGE
Attaching a Tow Line	171
Pull-Out Service with a Tow Line	172
The Tow Line and a Fulcrum	163
The Three Steps in Attaching Chains	175
Convenient Way to Consult a Map	187
A Pleasant One-Night Camp Site	190
Map Showing Yellowstone National Park	194
Map Showing Highways Between National Parks	196
Map Showing Distribution of National Forests	198
Fishing Scene in the Canadian Rockies	204

The Motor Camping Book

THE MOTOR CAMPING BOOK

CHAPTER I

WHY WE MOTOR-CAMP

The Motor Car has Become a Gasoline Caravan

THE purpose of this book is to give a practical working knowledge of how to camp out along the way while touring in a motor car. The motorist who carries an adequate camping outfit achieves the greatest degree of travel pleasure and freedom. If, on the other hand, he is inadequately equipped, the motor camping trip may sometimes be a sorry experience. Whether the camping tour be a close to home week-end jaunt or all the way across the continent, the amount of pleasure derived is largely dependent upon the amount and nature of preparation before starting. That is why this book in great part is devoted to the subject of motor camping equipment.

Before tackling the concrete problems of this modern method of camping, let us hark back a few years. In our boyhood days there was a fund of romance in the colorful gypsy caravan that creaked slowly over the horizon toward our old home town and then made camp in a nearby grove. It was the spark that set a-crackling within us the fires of wanderlust. Why had not we youngsters been born gypsies so that we also could take to the long road in this easy-going, happy-go-lucky fashion? It was rank injustice that they of the tawny skin should be a race alone so favored.

The reason we felt so keenly about it was because we recognized in these gypsies kindred souls. The nomadic instinct for a free life in the outdoors world ran in our blood and had for generations. It will continue to do so until the end of time. It is a peculiar thing, this craving to discover unknown worlds, breathe new air. It is especially strong in the boy and he never outgrows it as a man. It may remain so dormant as to be hardly recognizable but it is there just the same. To gratify it now and then is to get the best out of life. This instinct is wholly natural and wholesome.

For many years I have meekly answered its call when opportunity offered but I have long since

WHY WE MOTOR-CAMP

given up all attempts to understand it. All I know is that with the approach of summer there comes an increasing yearning to set eyes upon far-off places at the end of the open road. This call when answered is usually termed, "a much needed vacation." In reality it goes far deeper than that. It is the gypsy call of nomadic ancestors.

In the old days, none of us followed the open road in the care-free manner of the gypsy himself. His way of going was wholly attractive but hardly practicable for ourselves. That was a thing we only wistfully dreamed about. We followed our nomadic impulses, to be sure, but our manner of going was something of a compromise. Our own open road was usually one hedged in by two steel rails which not a few times lead us to a country boarding house of uncertain quality. And as time, tides, and through trains stop for no man, so we flashed by green beckoning hills that called in vain. I understand that even to-day, there are some people who continue to travel on railroads and stop at hotels and country boarding houses.

There came a time when behold a modern miracle was performed. The motor car appeared upon the scene. On the heels of its magic-like development followed motor touring. Here was the nomadic instinct within us popping out in a brand-new form. It was a distinct step in the direction of the real gypsy way but still something of a compromise. We were now following the open road, to be sure, but the smouldering camp fire in front of the silent tent was notably lacking from the picture. We were gypsies in the daytime but evening found us back in the turmoil of city streets.

There was still something of railroad-like schedule about such touring. If, off on a tour of some length, one had to regulate his movements so that night would find him in the neighborhood of a hotel. It detracted much from the pleasure of a motor tour when one was forced to spend a good part of a smooth running, gorgeous afternoon planning to make suitable connections with a given hotel. Strangely enough, even recently I have seen motorists on the road traveling from one hotel to another—not many in the West but still a number in the East. Hotels may be located on the open road but they are not a part of it. They belong to the city.

Besides, the matter of expense was no small item in touring of this sort. Hotel and garage keepers are in business to make money. Which is a worthy enough ambition but one likely to have a somewhat flattening effect upon the pocketbook of the average motorist. Until recently, touring was a luxury which not every motorist could afford.

In due time a happy and quite obvious solution sprang up in the West and quickly spread throughout the country. This was motor camping. You take along your own hotel and set it up by the roadside wherever night overtakes you. It is the real gypsy way. The motor car has become a gasoline caravan. Time and space are at your beck and call, your freedom is complete, and the expense need hardly be more than living at home.

In this motor camping, we are going the gypsies one better. The mileage that can be covered and the nooks and corners of the earth one can explore are practically unlimited. A cross-continent-tour from the Atlantic to the Pacific has become an every-day occurrence. What matters it if night finds one in the center of an expansive desert many miles from the nearest hotel? In five minutes you set up a hotel of canvas that is much more satisfying than any builded of brick and stone. You discover wonderful byways which he who travels by rail will never know and over which the motorist who depends upon hotels dares not venture.

The motor camping method of touring is both the newest and oldest method in the world.

Although one may wonder at its enormous growth during the past few years, this growth is not surprising for the reason that the idea is based upon one of the most fundamental instincts in the world—the gypsy call to the open road and the gypsy way of going. As part of this, might be included the wish to get the greatest amount of fun for the smallest expenditure of money.

Some motor tourists who continue to depend solely upon hotels because they are perfectly able to pay the prices, regard motor camping simply as a means of saving money. This is far from being the case. Anyone noticing the numerous tent- and bed-laden cars along the open road will find that a considerable proportion of these are machines of expensive manufacture—for example, Packards and Pierce-Arrows. It is reasonable to suppose that their owners are men of some means. These people realize that to camp beside a trickling trout stream, smoke their pipes of peace before a glowing fire, and then roll in for the night to the music of the stream and woods is a privilege of no small importance.

In regard to expense, it is safe to say that anyone who can afford a car and a vacation can likewise afford a motor camping trip. With these two requisites at your disposal a trip of this sort is

WHY WE MOTOR-CAMP

the most economical way in which one can go. There is no other method of travel whereby one can cover great distances and see such variety of country in a short time for so small a money outlay. Of course there is the initial outlay for the camping outfit but this soon pays for itself and is good for several years. If the car is in top-notch shape before starting, the only other necessary expenses are gasoline, oil, and the food you eat.

Indeed, motor camping is the only way in which many people can afford to travel at all. Otherwise, they would be forced to stay at home. I have seen many instances of this. For example, I recall meeting in Banff, Canada, a farmer with his wife and five children who were enjoying the marvels of the Canadian Rockies. Their car was a trifle ricketty in spots but it had brought them safely all the way across the broad Canadian prairies. They had camped out every night and would continue to do so until their return. This farmer explained to me:

"I've been wanting to bring my family out and show them this country for years but I couldn't stand the expense till I got the flivver. Going this way don't cost much more than living at home."

This farmer's case was fairly typical. There were fully twenty-five more of his sort in the motor camping grounds at Banff who might have made the same reply. And camped beside him in a tent attached to the side of a high-powered, costly car was an American whom I later learned was rated at quite a few hundred thousands of dollars in the banking circles of his home State. This man was equally as typical of motor camping.

CHAPTER II

THE IMPORTANCE OF RIGHT EQUIPMENT

Don't Wait till the Last Minute

THE call of the open road is a difficult matter clearly to define but the manner in which our gasoline caravans may be equipped to answer the call is a real and extremely definite problem. There is nothing intangible about this.

If possible, this problem should be completely solved weeks before the start of the trip. When the camper allows everything to slide along till the last day, he is likely to regret his lack of forethought. The need for articles overlooked, the bother of unnecessary things thrown in at the last minute, clumsy packing, unequal distribution of weight; these and a dozen more petty annoyances cropping up continually will detract greatly from the pleasures of the trip. One goes camping to have fun, not to be annoyed. This applies both to the periodical week-end camper and the party starting out upon a continuous two or three month's tour. In the case of the week-ender, once a satisfactory outfit is collected for his particular purpose, this then becomes a standardized system so that he can always attach his equipment to the car and drive away on a moment's notice.

Of course, one can go motor camping without any special regard to forethought. You can fling on the rear seat of the car, a shelter tent, armful of blankets, and cooking kit and call it a camping trip. It is. Furthermore, some campers have mighty good fun in spite of slack methods. But the type of motor camping to which I refer is something more than this. It is camp life with as many of the comforts of home life as are conveniently possible. The average motor camper is not a backwoodsman who when night overtakes him, sometimes curls up on the ground under a tree and rolls off to sleep. This motorist is accustomed to home comforts and there is no reason why he should not enjoy a number of these even when leading the gypsy life.

I would like to correct an erroneous and altogether too general impression about camping. Some people honestly believe that camping represents deprivation and hardship. To them, a camper is a queer being closely akin to a savage who takes an unholy joy in being as uncomfortable as he possibly can; he just dotes on sleeping upon a rock pile, running short of provisions, and getting drenched to the skin when opportunity offers.

As a matter of fact, such a camper is a wholly mythical character. Your true camper will put up with all these little inconveniences if fate so dictates, and he will smile in the bargain but he finds slight pleasure in them. He wants to sleep as comfortably and eat as heartily as anyone. Furthermore, if he is living in a well-equipped camp, the chances of such untoward happenings are very slight. Camp life when properly conducted is not "roughing it."

Speaking of camping in general it may be said that comforts vary to a great extent with the particular type of camp life one is living. If you have some means of transportation to carry your equipment you are so much better off than the hiker who packs all his worldly camping goods on his back. So far as a camp which is more or less constantly on the go, that of the motorist may easily be made about the most comfortable of all.

The problem of the man walking with a pack on his back is fairly simple. He knows his limitations. If he carries more than a given weight, he will be uncomfortable and the pack will become a nuisance.

The motor camper's problem is more complex. At just what stage the motor car's pack becomes a nuisance is sometimes difficult to define. A motor car can stand more than a human back but still it has its limitations. Excessive weight impairs efficiency. A car has lungs and springs. It may balk if good nature is driven too far; or the passengers may balk at being cramped for room. Provided everything is packed properly and in spite of this certain articles which were brought along as added comforts turn out to be burdens, then these should have been left behind. Added comfort while in camp hardly compensates for discomfort when traveling.

I can think of no other single kind of camping in which there are so many totally different types of equipment used as are to be found in motor camping. The manufacturers of these varied outfits are not notable for their bashfulness. Each will assure you that his particular make of tent, bed, or stove, as the case may be, is the finest in all creation and to use any other would bring you to grief. Now, when the man who makes a light tent weighing only seven pounds shouts this into one of your ears while the manufacturer of a seven-hundred-pound trailer bombards the other, you are conscious of a slight divergence of opinion—six

IMPORTANCE OF RIGHT EQUIPMENT 13

hundred and ninety-three pounds of divergence in fact.

Later in your travels you may meet actual users of these respective shelters and oddly enough each is likely to be as keen about his particular outfit as the man who made it. One says "go light" while another man says in effect "go heavy." Somebody must be wrong, you think. Of a dozen totally different kinds of tents, every one can't be the best.

None of these sponsors of varied outfits are wholly wrong and some are pretty close to right. The truth of the matter is that no article of equipment ever built answers all requirements. It all depends upon which phases of an outfit you want most and which seems to fit your particular needs best. It will never be possible for anyone to evolve a motor camping outfit which meets all requirements—that is, not so long as there are several hundred different makes and styles of motor cars to ride in.

Outfitting for a motor camping trip is a matter which requires individual judgment. Equipment which is suitable for one car may be totally inadequate for another. A motor camping outfit should be selected with great care. A dozen and one things must be considered: the power and capacity of the car, its hill-climbing capabilities, suitable sleeping arrangements, running-board capacity for carrying duffle, whether spare tires are carried on side or rear, proper distribution of weight so that the strain on springs will be equalized, these are but a few of the numerous items to be considered.

Sometimes this matter of selection takes years of actual experience before a man finds exactly what he needs. A short time ago I met a motor camper who for three years had constantly been changing various details of his outfit. He assured me that at last he had an outfit which suited him perfectly. As he checked over the list I realized that there were only a few items of which I, for my part, fully approved. So there you are. Motor camping is an individual problem that must be solved by the individual. I have examined the outfits of a good many different motor campers on the road and I have yet to find two alike in every respect. This is as it should be. There is so much leeway and flexibility to this kind of camping that most hard and fast rules other than a man makes for himself are out of the question.

On the other hand, there are certain fundamentals which all outfits should have in common. Chief among these is compactness. This does not

IMPORTANCE OF RIGHT EQUIPMENT

mean that one sacrifices comfort. Indeed, quite the contrary. Imagine, for example, three cooking pots very nearly of the same size. Why have them take up the space of three when it is just as easy to get a nested set in which one pot fits inside of the other?

I have seen motor camping cars on the road so bulging with equipment that they closely resembled moving vans. Bulk, more than weight has been the main fault in many such instances. I have seen other cars carrying fully as much weight and equipment but the various articles have been selected wisely in respect to compactness and packing ability. As a result of such careful preparation all the passengers in a car of this sort are perfectly comfortable and the appearance of the outside of the machine, except for a few small unobtrusive bundles, is no different than usual.

Only necessities should be included in the outfit —articles for which there will be definite use. I mean this in a relative sense. It is easy enough to define bare necessities such as bed, blankets, and toothbrush but presently you come to a border line across which lies a huge stack of articles which would be mighty nice to have along but may not be absolutely essential. Here is where good judgment comes in. Remember the mileage you will lug these articles and the number of times they will be packed and unpacked. There may be a folding table or chair which you consider quite essential to camp comfort; in which case it is very likely worth while taking such an article, providing the burden of carrying it is not too great.

The tendency of most motor campers starting out for the first time is to carry more equipment than they have definite use for. They presently find that they can be more comfortable through the elimination of many useless articles. It would be quite futile for me to attempt to define just what constitutes necessities for comfort in a motor camping trip. Two people traveling alone in a touring car might carry a tonneau full of necessities which in another car filled with passengers would be almost entirely eliminated. It all depends upon circumstances.

In the following pages of this book are described most of the different kinds of outfits used in motor camping. Very often, a given article may, on the one hand, be essential or on the other wholly inadequate, depending entirely upon what the individual motor camper wants and needs most. Through wise selection and discerning elimination I think it possible that you may be able to build

This shows a whole-souled morning stretch and likewise a combination bed and tent outfit used extensively in motor camping. The bed head is attached to the running board and the ridge of tent to the car top.

IMPORTANCE OF RIGHT EQUIPMENT

up the outfit which is most suitable for your particular purpose.

The intent of this book is to give practical information. In order to make this as definite as possible I have purposely called many of the manufactured articles by their right names instead of covering them in bewildering generalities for fear of giving a little free advertising. It has always seemed to me that one of the most difficult things in the world to get is plain, definite, unadorned information. This is what I attempt to give to the best of my ability.

CHAPTER III

THE CAR AND THE PACK

Distribution of Load—Tonneau and Running-Board Packing—Definite System—The Case of the Suit Case—Proper Covering and Lashing—The Baby Crib—Running-Board Guards and Carriers

If two motor campers have a whole touring car all to themselves, the solution of the packing problem is quite simple. The empty tonneau is the logical storeroom for the greater part of the equipment. When there are four, five, or six campers in the party, as is usually the case with a touring car, the storeroom possibilities of the tonneau become proportionately limited.

There are few things which detract more from the pleasure of motor car travel than a tonneau so cluttered up with equipment that the passengers are cramped for room. Some motorists feel so keenly upon the subject that they insist upon keeping the interior of the car free of all articles which belong strictly to the camping department

THE CAR AND THE PACK 19

of the trip. Of course, a good deal depends upon the size of the tonneau, but I think on the whole this is going a little too far. Even with a passenger-filled car, the interior can handle a certain amount of equipment without interfering with the comfort of anyone. It takes close and careful figuring, however. There is always room under the rear seat for a fair amount of equipment; perhaps two folding cots, each on end can be attached to the back of the front seat without being in anybody's way; a camp grate can be unobtrusively poked under the floor mat; possibly you will find that either a nested cooking set or a food box serves as an acceptable foot stool.

Packing of this sort is almost entirely dependent upon circumstances but in any case it is wise to call a halt before the thing goes too far. The moment the domain of the passengers seems to be infringed upon is the time to begin figuring out the possibilities of the outside of the car.

The luggage carried outside is likely to count up in weight and bulk, so due care must be given to wise distribution. For one thing, the strain upon the car springs must be fairly well equalized. A number of weighty pieces of duffle packed on the left running board may make the car sag in a way which it should not be allowed to do. This can very often be overcome by the addition of a luggage carrier attached to the rear, thus leaving one running board which is free of all luggage. It must be remembered, however, that there are disadvantages in carrying an especially heavy load on the rear in that this is likely to rack the car when traveling rough roads.

As a matter of fact, it would be quite futile for me to attempt any blue-print diagram of just how and where you are to pack your equipment. The fundamentals in all cases are: comfort of passengers, compactness of equipment, and ample protection against rain and dust, together with security in attachment, and easiest running conditions for the car. All these results may be arrived at in totally different ways, dependent upon varied circumstances. Spare tires carried on the side may give rise to a wholly different system of packing than when they are carried on the rear; a runabout or roadster with limited running-board space but having a fair-sized compartment under its rear deck will be packed differently from a touring car with its long running board. Every man needs to work out his own best system.

This system, whatever it may be, should be definitely decided upon at the start of the trip and if satisfactory should be strictly adhered to

THE CAR AND THE PACK

every time the car is packed while on the road. Certain known articles should always go to make up a certain pack and this should always be carried in the same place on the car. A definite system of this sort facilitates matters all around. The car will do its best, and furthermore, hectic mix-ups in packing every time one breaks camp, are obviated. Everything runs quickly and smoothly. If you want something in one of the packs while on the road, you know just where to lay hands on it.

In various kinds of camping trips other than motor camping, certain kinds of luggage bags are entirely unsuitable. For example, a suit case is not tolerated for a minute by the canoeist or tramper. Soft, rounded packs are the rule with these particular outdoors' men. Motor camping is more tolerant in this respect. Roll packs are wholly suitable on the motor car but so may flat and sharp-cornered ones be as well. The construction of the motor car is such that it permits a considerable amount of versatility so far as packs are concerned without sacrificing any due amount of compactness. There are quite a few flat surfaces upon which it is very often wise to lay other flat surfaces, even in preference to round. I know of motor campers who will not permit a duffle roll on the car. They hold that it is much better to pack bedding and most other equipment, flat. In such cases, the blankets are usually laid upon the back seat. When this method is used it is wise to enclose the bedding in a sheeting or canvas envelope.

In regard to suit cases I may say that I have always been in favor of them so long as I do not have to carry one. The suit case is really a trunk and a trunk is an article which I choose to have transported by other means than by hand. When one walks with as much baggage as a suit case contains the logical place to carry it is upon your back. Hence, the back pack sack. Considered as a trunk, the suit case may serve as a valuable luggage carrier on a motor camping trip. A duffle bag will hold more clothes but it will not take as good care of them.

If it came to a choice between a suit case and a duffle bag on a motor camping trip, I personally would choose the duffle bag. The reason is that I wear old clothes from the start to finish of a camping trip and any of these poked away in a duffle bag cannot possibly look worse when they come out than they do already. Women are likely to feel differently about it. A suit case is perfectly allowable.

THE CAR AND THE PACK

As a rule, you see more suit cases among motor campers of the East than those of the West. Clothing is the main reason for this. In the West, motor camping is an accepted institution, wherever you go. Everybody does it. When you drive through the streets of a large city togged in outing clothes nobody so much as lifts an eyebrow, even in spite of the fact that the women in the party very likely are clad in khaki riding breeches. In the East, on the other hand, a motor camping party is likely to dress up a bit when it strikes the streets of a city.

If one plans to take along a number of suit cases and doesn't care how he spends his money, the most suitable outfits perhaps are the suit case trunks which may either be bolted to the running board or attached to a rear luggage carrier. These have a capacity for three or four suit cases and are very well made. They are rain and dust proof. Such outfits, however, seem to be used more by motorists who stop at hotels than by those who camp out. The average motor camper who takes suit cases at all, rarely has more than one or two. These should be fully as rain and dust proof as those in the specially made trunks. Dust, rain, and mud will work their destructive way inside unless precautionary measures are taken.

Extra coverings are essential if a case is to be carried either on the running board or rear.

A suitable covering may be a sheet of oilcloth, rubberized canvas, a rubber blanket, pantasote or some similar material carefully wrapped around the case. Special covers can be bought in luggage stores which may answer at times but not in all instances. For this reason the following instructions from *Motor Age* of how to make a cover at home may be found worth while:

"A good black waterproof cloth should be used and the diagram shows the number of pieces needed and their shape. The best way is to make paper patterns for them by marking around the suit case. Allow enough on the edges so they can be hemmed by a machine.

"The sides and bottoms are made in one piece with the ends sewed in. The cover is made in the same way and should extend down the other part some distance. Curtain fastenings can then be sewed on the cover and lower portion for snapping on the cover. This is one of the easiest types of covers to make.

"Another way would be to leave a flap on one of the side pieces and bring it down over the top, fastening it in place on the other side. In this case the end pieces must be left with a flap also to be tucked in over the top of the suit case before the flap is brought down. There is a little more chance of dust getting into the suit case with this

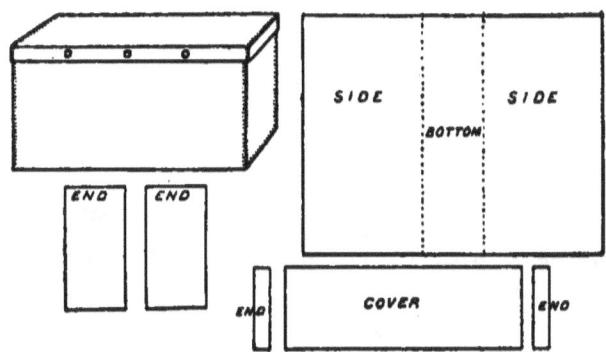

Diagram showing the number of pieces needed to make a suit case cover. The upper left hand drawing shows the completed cover.

type as there is not the protection afforded as when the cover slips over the sides and ends.

"If desired, the cover can be made to accommodate two suit cases by making it larger. When suit cases are strapped to the running boards the same straps often can be made to hold the covers in place, also doing away with the curtain fasteners."

Duffle or dunnage bags are used variously for carrying clothing, bedding, and food. It is allowable to pack both clothing and bedding in the same bag but food when carried in this way should have a bag by itself. There are numerous kinds and sizes of duffle bags. Some are waterproof while others are not; in one type the opening is along the side while in another it is at the end. A waterproofed bag with an end opening which has an extension canvas throat sewed in is usually preferable. Also, some bags have strap loops near each end. When carrying the bag on the running board, these may prove valuable little safeguards in preventing the lashings from slipping off.

The best size for a duffle bag depends upon personal liking and adaptability. Some people prefer two or three small bags instead of one large bag in order that there may be a convenient division of the equipment. There are times, however, when a single large bag may be even more convenient. Something of a happy combination of the two is found in a Gold Medal carrier patterned after the "diddy" bags used in the Navy. This is quite different in some respects from the usual type of duffle bag. It is really two canvas barrels telescoping, one into the other. Each of these barrels is thirty-six inches long. This is the ordinary length of the bag. It can be extended, however, in such a way that its length at full capacity is sixty inches.

If suit cases are carried, duffle bags may not be necessary. In such instances, clothing and personal effects are likely to be packed in suit cases, food in a box of some kind, and bedding wrapped securely in canvas, oilcloth, or rubber sheets. Each tent and cot will be confined within its individual canvas cover. If your tent has a detachable ground cloth, this canvas floor may serve as covering for some of the equipment. Of manufactured blanket roll covers, one of the most easily handled I know about is a Burch cover of twelve ounce khaki duck, five by six feet in size and especially equipped with ropes for facility in packing. It is not waterproofed, which may be something of a drawback, but when you have duck of this weight and quality you are reasonably safe.

All packs carried on the outside of the car should be both individually and collectively water, dust, and mud proof. I mean by this, that after the bundled up packs are apportioned in most suitable fashion on the running board or rear luggage carrier there should be an added safeguard in the form of a large sheet of waterproof material which covers them all. Before lashing down it is wise, when practicable, to run this sheet under as well as over the collective load, otherwise, water and mud from the wheels may work up from beneath.

Even when all the luggage is carried in the tonneau, due precautionary measures must be taken. I have a friend who once went camping this way and upon reaching the end of a day's run he discovered that a suit case full of belongings had jounced out of the tonneau without his knowing it. He never found it again. After that, he kept things pretty firmly lashed down. A dust and rain proof cover should be used for tonneau luggage as well as that on the running board. A canvas or oilcloth cover stretched from the back of the front seat to the top of the rear and held by cords or button hole arrangements answers very well. Ordinary oilcloth will be found valuable in many ways for packing.

There is one luggage carrier which is such a unique departure from those commonly used in motor camping that I think it worthy of mention. This is an outfit known as the Duluth Autopack. Logically enough, the idea comes fresh from the North Woods—the land of pack sacks. The Autopack is nothing more than a large-sized edition of the pack which the woodsman carries upon his back.

This carrier is a canvas pack three feet long,

THE CAR AND THE PACK

two feet high, and nine inches deep. The bottom rests on the running board. At the top are two felt padded hooks which fit over the side of the car. These hooks are both detachable and adjustable. The pack is entirely independent of the car but holds its place perfectly when attached. A surprisingly large amount of luggage can be carried in one of these bags.

As another example of the versatility of the motor car in shouldering packs, I might site the case of the car baby crib. Motor camping is a sport for all ages. It is a family affair. Six and eight months' old babies are common participants. As I review a western trip which I took recently, it seems to me that about one out of every half dozen motor camping parties I met was accompanied by a baby in arms.

In most cases of this sort there was a suspended hammock or crib in the tonneau for carrying the baby while traveling. These arrangements appeared to prove eminently satisfactory both for the mother and baby. A device of the kind which strikes me as being especially practical and comfortable for all concerned is the Gordon motor crib.

This outfit is suitable only for a touring car or a closed car (this is true of practically all baby carriers). It is attached to the back of the front seat and the floor of the tonneau. Underneath is a spring and above a suspension arrangement which together counteract the jolting of the car. This crib when not in use folds flat against the back of the front seat, or it can be taken out entirely. Even when occupied by the youngster, there is plenty of room for passengers in the back seat and the doors are not obstructed in any way.

In regard to the carrying of running board luggage in general, it may be said that the favorite manner of securing luggage in place is through liberal application of clothesline generously applied up, down, and across. By and large, this is perhaps the best and safest method. Its technique, however, is not always above criticism. On many cars I have seen rope used in a manner warranted to make a sailor or anyone else accustomed to the uses of rope, tear his hair in rage. Crazy quilt lashings are by no means the most secure. A slovenly packed car is much more noticeable and unwelcome to the eyes of a passerby than a well-packed one literally caked with mud or dust.

One often sees camp outfits which are held in place by guards of one sort or another along the outer edge of the running board. A method some-

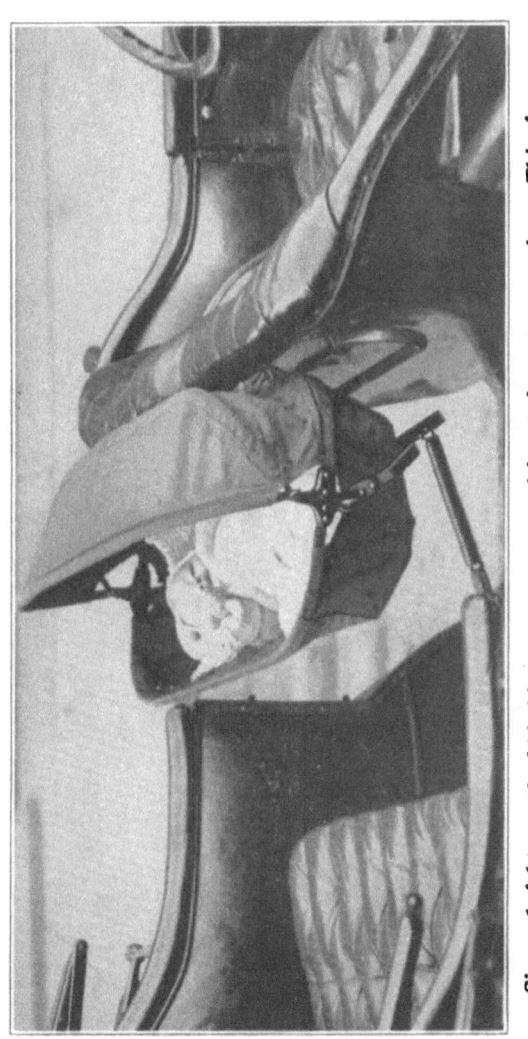

Six- and eight-month-old babies are common participants in motor camping. This shows a car crib with a spring and suspension arrangement which counteracts jolting.

times used is that of running two iron rods from fender to fender, a foot or so apart and parallel to the outer edge of the board. The rods are held in place at the ends by bolts fastened to the fender flanges. Much the same result can be arrived at with a board of wood, about one foot wide and sawed at each end to fit the angle of the front and rear fenders. In either case, luggage must be lashed down with rope as well, and protected properly against rain and dust. Side guards of this sort, although not always necessary, may represent just so much added security.

The Standley, the Rust, and the Marquette, luggage carriers are manufactured outfits built upon the same principle as the home devised fender to fender rods. In these instances, it is unnecessary to drill any holes for attachments. Three or more hand-screw clamps along the outer edge of the running board are the means of holding the frame in place. It is open to question whether or not such a device is as secure as one which is permanently bolted. I sometimes have an uneasy feeling that the jouncing of the car will work the clamps loose—although I have never heard of a clamp that really did come off. These outfits are used quite extensively by motor campers and seemingly with thorough satisfaction.

Each of these devices is detachable, adjustable, and collapsible. The Standley outfit, for example, is a folding metal frame which can be either extended or contracted to suit the length of the packages on the running board. A worth-while feature is a right angle inward extension of the frame at each end, so that the luggage is enclosed on all sides. As regards the Rust outfit, a commendable feature is a short rod at each end attached to the top of the running board, this, for added security.

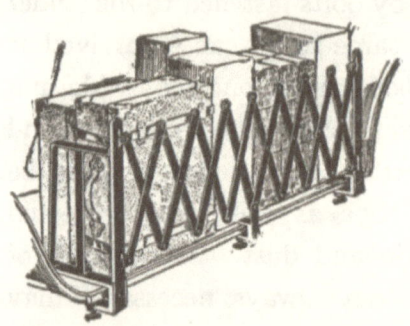

The luggage on the above running board is hardly that of a motor camper but the drawing shows the usefulness of a folding carrier.

As to whether or not rope lashings are necessary in connection with one of these carriers depends mostly upon the amount and type of luggage one carries and the bumpiness of the roads traveled. Rope never does any harm and it often does a lot of good. In any case, after the screw clamps have been attached by hand, the screws should be given an extra turn with the wrench.

THE CAR AND THE PACK 33

Either suit cases or duffle bags can be carried with this type of carrier. There is another sort of outfit, however, whereby the same luggage can be carried quite as securely, almost to the total elimination of a frame. The same type of screw-clamp running-board attachments are used and for this reason perhaps the uneasy feeling I have mentioned is still present. But they seem to work, and that is the important thing. In this type of outfit, the luggage is secured by two heavy web trunk straps attached to steel bars and these in turn clamped to the running board. The straps completely encircle the luggage in the same general manner in which they run around any ordinary suit case or trunk.

There are several outfits of this nature, although these may be said to fall into two classes. In one case the device

A bracket carrier which extends above the running board.

is a metal bracket which extends vertically

above the edge of the running board. The lower end is clamped to the board. Two of these brackets are used, one near each end of the luggage; more can be added if needed. Each bracket has a sliding up and down adjustment. The other class of outfit differs mainly in that the sliding bar rests crosswise on the running board. There is no side bracket in this instance. Adjustment is by width instead of height. Some motorists will find the former most suitable, others the latter, depending largely upon the nature of the luggage.

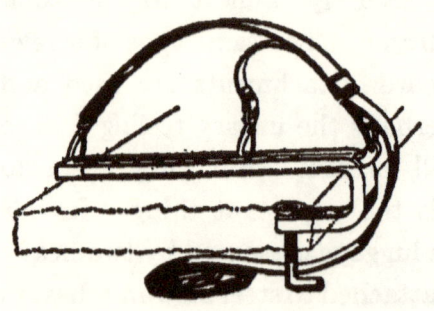

A bar carrier which rests crosswise on the running board.

All told, I consider these strap devices more practicable for motor camping purposes than the folding metal frame type. Both packing flexibility and security go with good web straps. Furthermore, these are more closely akin to duffle bags and other kinds of luggage which a camper carries.

CHAPTER IV

WATER CONTAINERS

Beware of Polluted Water—Alkaline Water—The Milk Can Plays a New Part—Water Bags—Running Board Canteens—Canvas Pails—Washbasins—Bathtubs

MY camping partner, whoever he happens to be, usually accuses me of being mighty fussy about drinking water. I realize that he is right about it but I was not always so. A few years ago while in the Near East I saw typhoid fever raging broadcast. Impure drinking water was the main reason. I have seen what pollution in water can do and have never quite forgotten it.

Fortunately, widespread conditions of this sort do not exist in this country. At the same time, one who travels and sips water as he goes is never absolutely free from the danger of typhoid. This is especially true in the case of the motor camper. So I say, beware of polluted water. Remember that not every sparkling brook trickling down a wooded hillside to the highway below is beyond reproach. A short time ago I started climbing a hill of this sort to find the source of such a brook. I presently quit the stream in disgust for it lead me directly through a refuse heap at the back of a summer hotel.

Unless you know the full life history of a stream, it is best to avoid its waters for drinking purposes. Shun, also, the well of the deserted farmhouse. Even the well of an occupied farmhouse will oftentimes stand close scrutiny. If the drainage from the house or outbuildings is toward the well, it is distinctly in the questionable class. See to it that the natural drainage is away from the water supply. A bubbling spring along the roadside is usually quite safe. In any case, however, if there is any doubt about your supply of drinking water, the simple process of boiling will render it incapable of giving typhoid. Small filter pumps are sometimes taken on camping trips but I do not think that these are especially effective. Boiling is best.

The eastern motorist who is spanning the continent for the first time is likewise warned against the alkaline water found in many sections of the West. This water may be pure enough so far as disease germs are concerned but a cupful will give one a serious case of cramps. Horace Kephart, an unquestioned authority on camping matters says that one teaspoonful of hydrochloric acid added to a gallon of alkaline water neutralizes it so that it becomes drinkable. I have never tried this but in any case I think I prefer to carry my own supply of sweet water gathered from other parts. You can usually recognize alkaline water some distance away without tasting it. There is a white deposit around the edge of the pond or lake.

Plenty of pure water carried in a suitable container is very often a matter of vital importance to the motor camper. For example, it would not be an especially pleasing experience to break down in the desert country west of Salt Lake City with not a drop of water in sight and parched throats and radiator both gone dry. I know one man who crossed the desert with only a small canteen. When he went back, he was very careful to take a generous supply of water along.

Locality, of course, has a great deal to do with how the motorist's water supply is managed. In many parts of the East, good water is so plentiful that a small canteen or folding water bucket may be all the equipment that is needed. To go so scantily supplied in alkali sections of the West would be foolhardy. When touring through the plains and desert country, it is advisable to have at least five gallons of good water on hand at all times. As the supply diminishes, fill it right up again at the first opportunity. In some parts of the Southwest, it is advisable to have fully ten gallons along.

One method of carrying water in fairly large quantities is by means of a five, eight, or ten gallon milk can strapped to the running board. Of course, if one were crossing the country from east coast to west it might be unwise to lug this can for a thousand miles and more when there was no immediate necessity for its use. You can wait until you strike alkali sections. Then, after buying a can, it might be well to drive around to the village blacksmith and have him fit it suitably to the running board.

Just how this is done depends upon the size of the can and the running-board space available. One way is to have three iron elbow brackets made with the top of each rolled over so that these will hold iron rings. These brackets, bolted to the running board a suitable distance apart and in form of a circle, serve as supports for the can. The can is held rigid by means of straps run across the top and anchored below to each of the respective iron rings.

WATER CONTAINERS

This milk-can arrangement may be perfectly practicable in some cases but it is likely to prove quite as impracticable and rather bothersome in others. I do not recommend it as the best method in the world. So far as general application is concerned, probably an easier way out is in the form of water bags of various sizes. If you live in the East, you may never have heard of the canvas water bag, but if your home is in the West you are wholly familiar with the water bag and its great usefulness. Among Westeners, a camping outfit is hardly complete unless it contains this piece of equipment. For years on end, the water bag has been an old standby among campers; surveyors, prospectors, and cattle men. The lonely gold prospector of former days setting out across dry areas with his slow-moving pack mule always carried a water bag. It is just as practicable to-day for the camping vacationist setting forth with his more speedy gasoline pack mule.

This article is sold by camp outfitters under various names such as "Egyptian," "South African," and "Desert" water bag but in all cases it is the same thing. It is nothing more than a rectangular-shaped bag of heavy duck with a bottle mouthpiece at one of the top corners. This is sealed with a cork stopper. Also, at the two top corners are rings for a rope to hang the bag up by.

In some instances, there is a faucet attachment at one of the corners so that the water-filled bag when hung up serves as a reservoir. For the most part, the main difference between various water bags is the construction of the top. The old-timer's bag was permanently sealed across the top so that the only opening was the bottle mouthpiece. Most of the bags used to-day seem still to be of this old-time type. Recently, however, several manufacturers have been making bags which can be opened all the way across the top. I consider this a distinct improvement. It makes the bag much easier to fill and clean and it is useful in various ways not possible with the closed top. For example, after a bag has been filled with water, a jar of butter or milk may be set inside. Thus, it does valuable service as a refrigerator.

Whatever the construction of the water bag may be, the manner in which it works is always the same. It is both a water container and a water cooler. The cold water which you pour into it remains at about the same frigid temperature for many hours even on the hottest days. No especially patented device is the reason for this. It is simply the way of nature. The process which

WATER CONTAINERS

keeps the water cool is slow and steady evaporation which is taking place through the pores of the canvas. You have working for you in the form of this bag, a natural refrigerator.

Water bags are made in various sizes ranging from one to five gallons. Whatever the size, a bag of this sort is of such great service in motor camping that I would be inclined to class it as a necessity. In cases where a fairly liberal supply of water needs to be carried in the car, I think that three two-gallon bags makes a happy combination —one for drinking, one for the radiator, and one for emergency.

The canvas water bag. It might be classed as a necessity for the motor camper.

The water in a properly handled water bag will evaporate slowly and harmlessly but it will neither leak nor drip. Now and then a bag does commit these little unpleasantries. This may mean that the bag has not been thoroughly soaked in water before using. This should always be done. Likewise, the bag when carried in the car should be suspended in some way so that its surface does not come into contact with anything. For this reason, neither the running board nor the side of the car are suitable places to carry it. Some motorists make the mistake of lashing a bag to the side of the car. The disastrous results are threefold: the water leaks out, that which remains becomes warm, and the constant chaffing of the wet canvas against the side rubs off the paint on the car, leaving ugly bare spots.

The best carrying arrangement as a usual thing is that of suspending the bags from the car top so that they do not come into contact with any other surfaces. Even in this way, they can be lashed to some extent by means of cords attached to the two lower corners. This prevents too much swinging.

As I have said, the water bag was in use long years before the motor car appeared upon the scene. The same may be said of the ordinary water canteen. But it was not until recently that a practical minded Californian combined the canteen and the motor car running board. Both the idea and its practical application are worthy of considerable admiration. I would not exactly call the canteen a substitute for the water bag but there are times when perhaps the two can be used together to advantage.

This type of running-board canteen is known as the Boyco. It is semicircular in shape and has a

WATER CONTAINERS

capacity for one, two, or three gallons of water according to the size of the respective outfit. In any case, the canteen is strapped and clamped to the running board. There are several different styles of outfits. In two of these, it is not necessary to disengage the canteen from its clamps when one wishes either to drink or wash. In one instance, there is a tilting device whereby only a strap is loosened and the water carrier is tipped down in a convenient way. The other outfit is unique in that it has two mouthpieces, one for the radiator and the other for yourself. That of the radiator is a long curved neck forming a spout. The other is a small faucet under which is placed a cup or wash basin. Of course, when the radiator gets thirsty, it is necessary to detach the canteen and carry it out front.

An interesting variation of the canteen idea is found in a Boyco outfit which consists of three canteens on the running board, side by side, and the whole row held together and to the running board by one set of straps and clamps. One of these holds gasoline, the next oil, and the third water. The gasoline container is painted a warning red and stenciled "gasoline," while the oil canteen is painted blue and also stenciled. The water can is enclosed in a blanket covering.

Hence, one is not likely to take a swallow of gasoline by mistake. Of course, one should take an extra supply of gasoline and oil on any long trip and there is much to be said in favor of this canteen method. We now come to water buckets. A bucket of some sort is necessary both in camp and upon the road. Let it be of the folding canvas variety. Any camp outfitter has quite an assortment of these. It is advisable to get one which has a spout of some kind so that it will be equally adaptable for camp use and filling the radiator. One or two pails of this order have spouts which are on the general lines of a tea kettle. In another type, the top rim of the pail converges to a blunt point on one side and forms a nose. In both types, there are a few buckets which have wire netting sewed across the spout to strain the water. This is a point worthy of consideration.

All things being equal, I like a canvas pail that is capable of standing rigidly on its own feet when

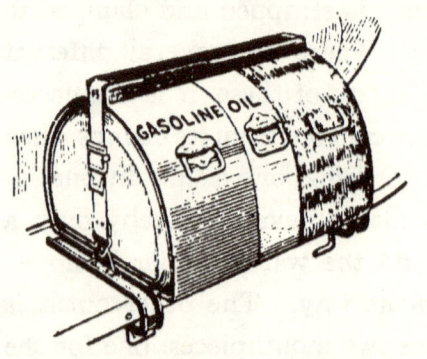

Gasoline, oil, and water, side by side on the running board.

Left photo: a folding canvas wash basin. Right photo: a rubber wash basin and stand.

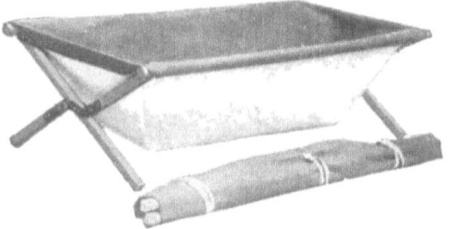

Portable bathtub for a "get in all over" bath. It folds to its length.

A rubber bathtub for a "stand up" bath. At the left, is shown the carrying case.

WATER CONTAINERS 45

filled with water without coyly shrinking together the moment it is set on the ground. A bucket which is braced on the sides with folding steel stays may usually be depended upon to stand upright. There is a canvas pail of this sort known as the Duplex which I like very well. There are two styles of this, one with spout and the other without. The former is the more suitable for motor camping. Likewise, it is provided with a strainer.

A folding canvas bucket with steel stays, a spout, and a strainer.

There is a Duplex folding canvas washbasin of the same steel construction as that of the pail but I do not care for this. It is well enough made; my great objection is, that the material is canvas. In any canvas basin, the soapy scum attaches itself to the fabric and is difficult to clean out. A rubber basin has the disadvantage of being rather wobbly but in my opinion it is more satisfactory. Furthermore, it folds into a very compact package. A number of basins of this sort are made of rubberized duck. This is perfectly suitable material.

A folding washstand is a rubberized duck basin with tripod-like legs added. Some motor campers use these. If one has plenty of room to spare, an added convenience of this kind may prove worth while but as a rule I think it means cluttering up the car with just one thing more that is not necessary.

At first thought, one may be inclined to place the folding bathtub in the same category. The average motor camper will find ample bathing facilities in lakes and streams. On the other hand, perhaps the motor camper is remaining for some length of time in a glacial stream country; there is plenty of water but he dares not venture into it. There are other times in motoring when a bath is not always easy to locate. Besides, it is good to have a hot bath now and then even where there are plenty of bathing streams about.

For a "get in all over" bath, the Gold Medal rubberized canvas outfit is perhaps the best. This is 5 feet long, 27 inches wide, and 16 inches deep when set up. It weighs 16 pounds and folds to 5 feet long by 5 inches square. Unless one is touring with a trailer, this is rather sizable luxury. For ordinary going, if one feels the need of taking a bathtub along at all, the ordinary folding rubber tub probably will be found suitable enough. Such an outfit is made in various sizes ranging from 16 to 32 inches in diameter and folds into a very small package.

CHAPTER V

THE COOKING KIT

Motor Luncheon Kits Versus Camp Cooking Kits—Nesting Outfits—Aluminum Ware—Steel Ware—Mixed Sets—Additional Kitchen Items—Frying Pans—The Vacuum Bottle

MOST any supply store will show the prospective motor camper an attractively arranged array of motor luncheon kits which at first sight may strike him as being a ready-made solution of the food utensils problem. To be sure, pots and pans are lacking from the average outfit of this sort but it includes a half dozen knives and forks, as many cups and spoons, pepper and salt cellars, and one or two vacuum bottles. There may even be a refrigerator. These various articles are all neatly enclosed in a suit case or running-board box.

Such an outfit fulfills exceedingly well the purpose for which it is intended. That purpose is to serve as a luncheon kit. But so far as motor camping is concerned, it is not likely to prove as suitable. It is not my intention to make a wholesale condemnation of such kits for motor camping. For example, when a party is on tour, it is usually advisable to have in the middle of the day a light lunch which has been prepared at breakfast time. In this way, a complete unpacking of the outfit becomes necessary only once a day and hence much time and labor is saved. A fairly small, unobtrusive lunch kit may prove very handy under such conditions. Let the motor camper be sure, however, that a certain kit is exactly what he wants and that it does not duplicate other parts of the equipment or add unnecessary bulk or weight to the carrying load.

I have no special objection to a suit case in its proper sphere but I think there are better methods for carrying cooking utensils. These are articles which should take up a minimum amount of space. The first thing to consider is compactness and nesting ability. There is no reason why a dozen utensils should take up more room than a single article. This eliminates at one fell swoop most of the favorite pots and pans which are used in the home kitchen. Utensils with side handles and ears are barred. Also, eating and cooking dishes should be considered, together, rather than as separate units. Perhaps my main objection to

THE COOKING KIT 49

the luncheon kits is that the two are regarded separately.

Many motor camping families select their cooking utensils from the home kitchen, quite regardless of packing ability. I do not wish to give the impression that a perfectly miserable time is the invariable result of such procedure. Such campers may and usually do get along well enough. But this is not the best method. The best method is the one whereby there is the greatest degree of comfort, averaging up all angles of the case. Taking motor camping as a whole, with its many diverse conditions, it may be said that cooking utensils can be more nearly standardized than in most sides of this recreation. That is, a given number of people are likely to need a given number of dishes whether they are gone for a week or a month, and the general types of dishes carried by various parties will be about the same.

To my mind, the most practical cooking outfit for motor camping is a single, compact nesting outfit which includes dishes, pots, pans, cups, knives, forks, spoons, in fact every utensil that is necessary with which to cook and eat a square meal. As to whether it is wisest for a camper to buy a ready prepared set of this sort or on the other hand, shop around town and build up his own set, is something of an open question. A personally conducted search of this sort often takes the aspect of working out a jig-saw puzzle but even so, it is not half bad fun.

There is a complete nested alumium outfit called Wear Ever which is quite a favorite among motor campers. Respective two-person, four-person, and six-person kits come ready packed, although sometimes the contents of a certain kit varies as sold by different outfitters. The various dishes, pots, and pans of a given set nest within each other so compactly that when not in use the complete outfit is only a trifle larger than the size of the largest pot. Over this fits a canvas cover.

If you have ever cooked with aluminum ware, you know something about its propensity for conducting heat. Some people consider this an advantage, others a disadvantage. It depends to a great extent upon the nature of the utensil. Aluminum cups, for example, have burned altogether too many unwary mouths to receive universal commendation. I would never for a minute include an aluminum cup in my outfit. One or two other aluminum articles about which I am not especially keen are fry pan and plates.

A two-person Wear Ever cooking set sold by some stores contains nineteen utensils and weighs

THE COOKING KIT

six pounds. The largest pot holds six quarts. The remaining utensils, with the exception of fry pan and plates, are confined within this pot. This outfit contains the following:

- 1 4-qt. Cooking Pot.
- 1 6-qt. Cooking Pot.
- 1 2¼-qt. Coffee Pot.
- 1 10½-inch Fry Pan.
- 2 1-pt. Bowls.
- 2 ¾-pt. Cups.
- 2 Plates.
- 1 Salt and Pepper.
- 2 Knives.
- 2 Forks.
- 2 Teaspoons.
- 2 Tablespoons.

A typical four-person aluminum set contains 35 utensils and weighs 10½ pounds. The contents of this are as follows:

- 1 7-qt. Cooking Pot.
- 1 9-qt. Cooking Pot.
- 1 11-qt. Cooking Pot.
- 1 2¼-qt. Coffee Pot.
- 2 8½-inch Fry Pans.
- 4 1-pt. Bowls.
- 4 ¾-pt. Cups.
- 4 Plates.

1 Salt and Pepper.
4 Knives.
4 Forks.
4 Teaspoons.
4 Tablespoons.

The six-person aluminum outfit is made up of 51 pieces and weighs 13½ pounds. This contains:

1 7-qt. Cooking Pot.
1 9-qt. Cooking Pot.
1 11-qt. Cooking Pot.
1 14-qt. Cooking Pot.
1 2¼-qt. Coffee Pot.
2 8½-inch Fry Pans.
6 1-pt. Bowls.
6 ¾-pt. Cups.
6 Plates.
2 Salt and Pepper.
6 Knives.
6 Forks.
6 Teaspoons.
6 Tablespoons.

There are other nesting cooking utensil sets sold by outfitters, these variously under the names of Armorsteel, Hardsteel, and other trade epithets. The foundation of these utensils is steel which is double tinned (except fry pan); for the sake of convenience I will call these steel ware. As in the

THE COOKING KIT

case of aluminum, there are respective two-, four-, and six-persons sets. These utensils correspond in shape and style to the aluminum but they are somewhat heavier in weight and the sizes of the respective utensils vary slightly. Aluminum ware, of course, is the more costly.

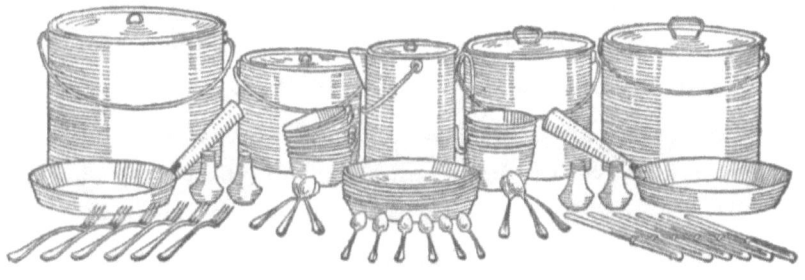

Upper drawing: a six person aluminum cooking outfit.

Lower drawing; how the above outfit looks when packed.

Both the alumnium and steel ware sets are exceptionally well made and any camper has reason to take justifiable pride in the possession of either. My particular choice, however, in a cooking outfit is something of a compromise. It is a nested set which is a conglomerate mixture of both these wares and likewise includes enameled ware, wood, and sometimes even tin. I favor aluminum cooking pots, steel fry pans, steel knives and forks, enameled ware dishes and cups, and a wood salt shaker. My preference concerning the salt shaker is due to the fact that the wood absorbs the moisture in the salt and thus gives the grains an opportunity to trickle out.

Anyone feeling as fussy as I do on this subject will be able to collect a mixed set of this sort which is reasonably compact. All the aluminum and steel ware utensils in the complete sets are sold separately and this is a distinct help. If you get a straight set of aluminum ware I urgently suggest that you substitute enameled ware cups for those of aluminum. This can be done without seriously disturbing the nesting capabilities of the set. I offer this mixed set idea only by way of suggestion. It is by no means necessary. Many experienced campers prefer the straight sets either of aluminum or steel ware.

In any case, the make-up of any one set of ware such as listed in the two- four- and six-person kits is more or less flexible. Certain conditions may call for elimination or substitution. For example, by refering to the four-person kit you will find three cooking pots listed. This is none too many for a wood fire but if a gasoline stove is used with its more limited cooking area, one of these pots perhaps may be unnecessary. Also, when there are

THE COOKING KIT

three, five, or seven campers in the party, suitable additions can be made. As a matter of fact, I think that all these sets are a trifle short on teaspoons, cups, and plates. In each set, one or two of each of these utensils could be added to advantage.

There are a few additional kitchen items which should not be forgotten. For example, a cooking spoon, a long-pronged cooking fork, and either a carving or good woods knife. And what would camp be without flapjacks? Don't forget the flapjack turner. Unless one finds it convenient to take along a bread pan, the largest cooking pot of a nested set will serve as a dish pan. Among other items might be mentioned: pot hooks, can opener, dipper, dish towels, soap, and a collapsible meat safe. The meat safe is a netting arrangement which looks something like a fish trap. Meat suspended inside of this netting is fly proof. This device may be hung up in the tent or from the limb of a tree.

The average motor camper will buy his food supplies as he goes but in instances where one drives off the beaten path so that a considerable amount of food is needed, the Abercrombie food bags are suitable containers. These consist of a number of small bags, each $8\frac{1}{2}$ inches in diameter which are laid one on top of the other in a nine-inch duffle bag. Rice, oatmeal, flour, baking powder, salt, and so on, are each confined to a separate bag. However, when friction-proof tins can be used to advantage these are oftentimes better containers for certain foods. Also, glass jars, when properly packed, are not to be scoffed at. I will take up this matter of food containers more fully in another chapter.

Frying pans, of course, are included in the cooking sets which I have described. This temperamental, romantic, and at the same time practical utensil plays such a prominent rôle in camp life that it deserves further mention. Until a few years ago the frying pan, because of its protruding handle, was something of a packing problem in camp outfits. Recently, a camp frying pan's chief boast has been that it is provided with a certain kind of detachable or folding handle. For camp use, a pan so equipped is far preferable to the kitchen variety.

The folding handle fry pan usually proves more satisfactory than the detachable. The folding handle outfits probably most used are the Miller and the American. In each case, when the utensil is packed, the handle folds back so that it fits flat on the bottom of the pan. The best size for a

This shows a folding handle fry pan ready for use and with handle folded back for packing. A stick can be inserted in the rings while cooking.

A wood salt shaker. The wood absorbs the moisture in the salt and thus gives the grains an opportunity to trickle out.

A vacuum bottle that can't be broken. There is no glass in it. The liquid container is made of steel. This particular bottle was run over by a heavy team. Except for dents it is as good as ever.

A friction top can is a handy container for carrying small supplies of tea, coffee, sugar, and other food.

CHAPTER VI

THE COOKING FIRE

The Fire and the Law—Burner Stoves—Alcohol—Kerosene—Gasoline—The Wood Fire—Folding Grates—The Reflector Baker—Wood Stoves

So far as a cooking fire is concerned I must express an extreme partiality for a lingering heap of glowing wood coals. Food that is broiled, baked, fried, or boiled in this true out-of-doors fashion seems to taste better and fit more suitably into nature's sphere of things than when cooked upon a man-manufactured stove. Yes, I like a wood fire to cook by. On the other hand, when it rains pitchforks and one is driven to tent shelter, a homely little black-faced stove that you can poke under your arm and take into the tent with you is a friend worth having.

A burner stove of some sort is of such great convenience in motor camping that it comes pretty close to being a necessity. For one thing, there are certain localities in the country where it is against

THE COOKING FIRE

the law to build a wood camp fire. Suppose you depend solely upon wood and have a fine camp fire blazing away when presently the town constable strolls in upon the happy scene and wants to know, by heck, what right you got to build a fire in a county where its stric'ly ag'n the law. The results are likely to be uncomfortable for all concerned.

Laws of this sort are not general, but like lightning, they often strike in unexpected places. If traveling through unfamiliar sections, it is just as well to inquire beforehand how matters stand in this respect. In parts of New England, for example, one county may have no objection to camp fires while the next prohibits them. Sometimes it is an easy matter to get a permit by applying to the town clerk or similar official.

In any case, one is playing it safe by taking along a burner stove, if only for emergency's sake. There is no objection whatever to the use of these. Even in localities where there is no law against wood fires, a farmer may raise a howl against a motorist camping on his property solely because of the fire risk. His objections are invariably turned to friendly consent immediately you tell him that you cook with a small stove.

I refer especially to small stoves in which the

fuel may variously be fluid alcohol, solid alcohol, kerosene, or gasoline. I will first take up the solidified alcohol type. In this case, the fuel itself burns. The most practical outfit of this sort for out-of-doors use is probably the Theroz stove. This looks like a small suit case and can be carried by a handle in the same way. It is a light, compact, and strongly built metal case 16 inches long, 8 inches wide, and 5 inches high, when set up.

How the Theroz type of solid alcohol stove looks when in use.

This stove has two burners and under each of these is placed a friction top can of fuel which goes with the outfit. The flame is not so hot as that of a gasoline stove but it gives good-cooking action. One can turn out appetizing flapjacks with this alcohol outfit and that in itself is a science which requires a fairly hot fire. In timing the burning life of a single can of Theroz fuel, I have found that it lives something over an hour with a steady flame. The unused portion of a can is put away for next time. The fuel remains solid even when

THE COOKING FIRE 61

burning; the fact that it does not leak or spill at any time is a point distinctly in its favor.

The operation of this outfit is extremely simple. There are no parts to get lost or out of order. One touches a match to a can of fuel; that is all there is to it. When the stove is not in use it does service as a container for additional cans of fuel and perhaps a certain amount of equipment. The concern which manufactures this stove makes another outfit called the Theroz Mess Kit. The mess kit is a good enough little device of its kind, but does not give the same service as the stove. The stove is better for motor camping.

The small fluid alcohol stoves are totally different from the solidified. Take, for example, the Universal single burner outfit. This converts denatured alcohol into gas and the flame is regulated like that of an ordinary gas range. This flame is hot enough to boil a quart of water in seven minutes. The alcohol is confined in a quart reservoir stationed a few inches above and at one side of the body of the stove. The body is circular in shape and has a grate which is $10\frac{3}{4}$ inches in diameter. This is large enough to accommodate any ordinary cooking utensil. The outfits weighs about ten pounds.

There are two stoves less expensive and much

lighter in weight than the Universal but operated on the same principle. They are smaller and cannot be expected to give the same service. These are respectively known as the Alpha and the Glogau. The former weighs two pounds and the latter only eight ounces. As a rule, I do not think that the fluid alcohol stove proves as satisfactory for camping purposes as the solidified alcohol, kerosene, or gasoline outfit.

Several small kerosene stoves used in camping are of Scandinavian extraction, notably those of the Optimus, Primus, and Jewel type. If you have read Nansen's *Farthest North*, you may recall flattering references to stoves of this sort. Of these three, the Optimus seems to be the one most readily obtainable from outfitters in this country, so I will briefly describe this.

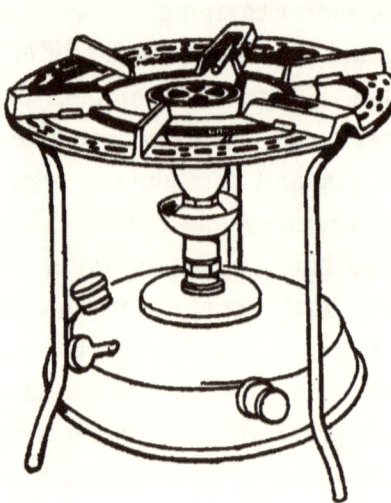

The Optimus type of kerosene stove.

The Optimus stove will boil a quart of water in

THE COOKING FIRE 63

three minutes. It is hardly necessary to remark further upon the intenseness of the flame. This is a blow torch pressure outfit something after the order of the kind used by the plumber when he comes around to mend the water pipes. When burning at its highest power the stove consumes a quart of kerosene in about six hours. The flame is regulated by turning a thumb screw. This stove is a single burner outfit eight inches high and weighing between three and four pounds. There are two styles, both of the same construction but one provided with a silent burner and the other with an outdoor burner. I like the silent better.

Not quite so hot a flame is found in another single burner outfit of about the same size, construction, and principle of operation, known as the Kero. This outfit, however, weighs only two pounds and a distinct advantage is the fact that it will burn gasoline as well as kerosene.

Most of the stoves so far described are single burner outfits and for this reason their sphere of usefulness is somewhat limited. The average motor camper can make better use of two burners because he wants hot drink and hot food at the same time. And at the end of a long day's run he is likely to demand both in a hurry. For two campers, say, who do not wish steady use, but merely a stove for emergency's sake, it is my opinion that an outfit of the Kero or Optimus type may come pretty close to filling the bill. For

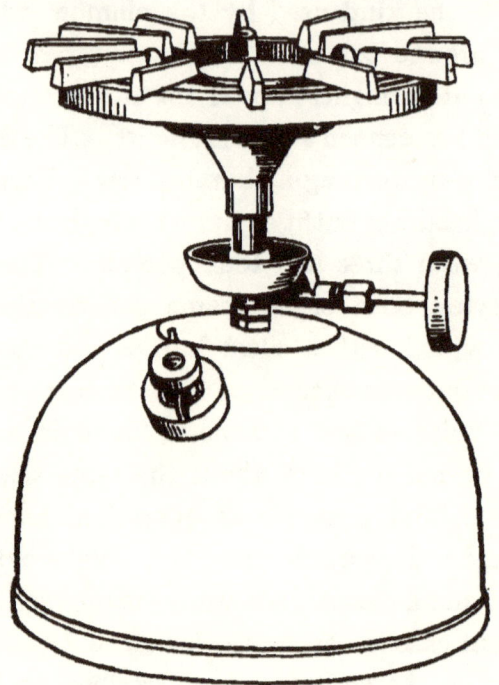

The Kero type of single-burner stove.

steady use or with a larger party, two stoves of this sort may be found advisable. And as against this, you have the compactly built single-unit, two-burner gasoline stove. Which of these alternatives to choose is something of an open question.

THE COOKING FIRE 65

This question is answered both ways, and seemingly to the eminent satisfaction of all concerned. I think it safe to say, however, that the two-burner gasoline stove is the cooking apparatus of the average motor camper who carries a burner outfit. This is certainly true, so far as my personal observation goes. A gasoline stove, in common with those just described, may be lacking in the element of camp-fire romance, but it unquestionably does the job which it undertakes with astonishing ease, directness, and effectiveness. Whenever I watch one of these little outfits at work I marvel at the businesslike way in which it tackles the problem of turning out a well-cooked meal.

I will go to some lengths in describing the operations of the two-burner gasoline stove. To fail to do so in a book upon motor camping would be akin to writing a treatise on motor cars without saying anything about their construction. The three camp gasoline stoves in general use are variously known as the American Folding Kampkook Stove, the Auto Kamp Kook Kit, and the Auto Camp Stove. My personal experience has been mainly with the American Kampkook outfit, so I will describe the construction of this particular stove. I have seen this outfit used more among motor campers than any other and they all seem to like it.

This stove when packed for carrying is to outward appearances nothing more than a black enameled case 14½ inches long, 8 inches high, and 3½ inches thick. There are no projecting parts; the complete works are confined within this case. The weight of the oufit is eight pounds.

In opening the stove for use you press against either end of the box directly below the cover. This disengages a rivet and the cover comes completely off. Make a slight turn in each corner of the case and four legs drop through the bottom and come rigidly to attention. The cover is then placed upside down on the ground or table and the stove laid upon it. On the open top of the stove above the burners rests a grate upon which are placed the cooking vessels.

To go into further detail, a, in the accompanying drawing, is the gasoline tank. This is detachable. When the stove is being carried, this is packed away inside the case. After lifting out the tank, the first operation is that of filling it and assembling the immediate parts. Letter b represents a cut-off valve and c a filler plug at the end of the tank. We first close this cut-off valve and then remove the filler plug, after which the tank is

THE COOKING FIRE 67

filled about three quarters full of gasoline and the filler plug is replaced and screwed down tightly.

The stove is operated under air pressure supplied to the tank. This pressure forces the gasoline to the generator tube where it is converted into gas

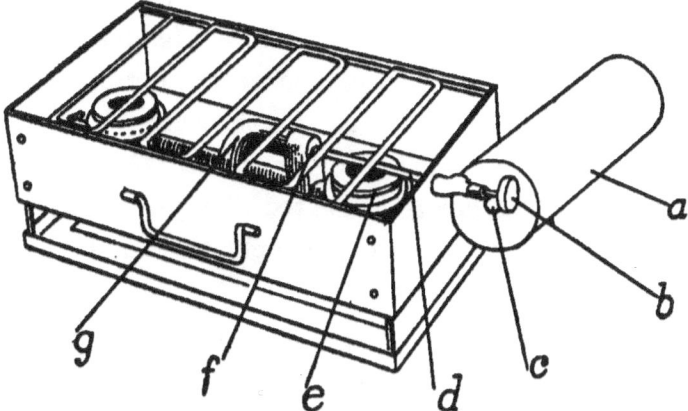

This drawing shows the various parts of the two-burner gasoline stove referred to in the text.

and fed to the burners. You attach a small air pump to a thumb screw on the filler plug and give the tank about a dozen strokes of air.

The method of generating the first burner is interesting. No alcohol torch is required to light it. Letter d represents the generator, f is the needle seat, and g the manifold casing. Letter e is the burner cap and in the center of this is a cup. This cup is filled with gasoline from the end of the generator, after which the tank, together with the generator, is placed in the proper position. The tank must be elevated from the ground or else the gasoline will not feed.

The gasoline in the burner cap is lighted and when this is nearly burned out you open cut-off valve *b* and the burner immediately ignites from the flame. It is necessary to generate only one burner. This produces gas for the second burner which may be turned on or off at will. After the second burner has been lighted, the cut-off valve on the tank is opened to supply the additional amount of gas required.

The tank holds enough gasoline to run both burners for two and one half hours when burning at full capacity. This means a clear blue flame devoid of soot or smoke and one which burns with intense heat. The flame may be turned to a low simmering fire when that is what one wishes. It may take an unduly long time to tell all about this stove in detail but the actual process of putting it to work is very quick and simple.

Of course, any piece of mechanism operated by gasoline has days off when it does not run fully up to form and this gasoline stove is no exception to the rule. The matter can usually be easily remedied. You may know by experience that

THE COOKING FIRE 69

the flame now and then becomes dull and sluggish. As a usual thing it is merely gasping for air. A little more pressure with the aid of the pump is sufficient. If this fails, the trouble is probably in the form of a particle of carbon or dirt which has become lodged in the orifice of needle seat f. This may be removed by opening and closing cut-off valve b quickly a number of times while the stove is in operation. If the flame goes out during this process, simply relight it with a match. In any case, after a gasoline stove has been used for some time, the generator and cut-off valve should be thoroughly cleaned.

As I have previously remarked, the heavens above and the law of man below permitting, I like a wood fire to cook by. I think that even the confirmed users of gasoline stoves (who are innumerable) will find it well worth while to fall back upon wood now and then. I will mention some few articles of equipment which may be used to advantage in connection with a wood cooking fire. By no means do I suggest that you load up with all of these but if there is room for only one, my choice would be a folding grate of some sort.

There are many different varieties of folding grates. The sort which folds perfectly flat is the type most used and about the easiest to carry. There are a number of interesting variations in this sort of grate. This grate in its simplest form is a rectangular shaped wire grid with a leg at each corner—nothing more. This may be either quite small or fairly large in size. Sometimes it is more convenient to carry two small grates than one large one of the same total cooking capacity. By placing the two small grates side by side over the fire the same amount of area is covered as in the case of the larger outfit.

A grate of this sort is primarily designed to serve as a resting place safely to hold pots and pans. It may also be used as a broiler but is not always trustworthy in this respect; an unwary chop may slip between the wires into the fire when one's back is turned. Strictly speaking, meat and fish should be cooked in the same sort of broiler as they are accustomed to at home. There are a number of camp grates which are especially designed to accommodate a broiler in addition to pots and pans, as for example, the Collis and the United outfits.

The United grate is somewhat out of the ordinary in that there is a separate under grid which is interchangeable in height. This may serve either as a support for the broiler or as a foundation upon

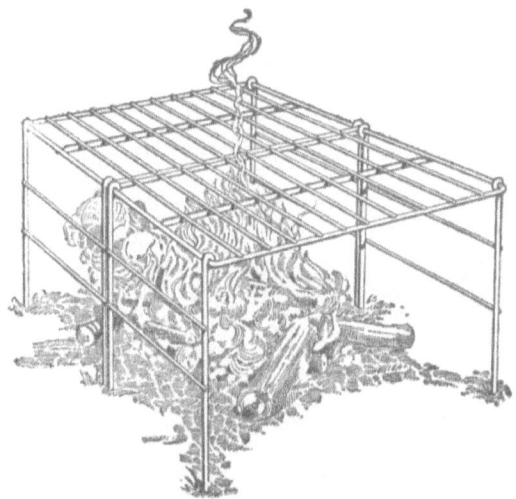

Two small grates placed side by side to give the same cooking area as a large one. Two small outfits are sometimes the easier to pack.

A grate designed to accommodate a broiler in addition to pots and pans.

which to build a charcoal fire. A good charcoal fire is a thing not to be scoffed at and this particular manner of laying one is about the most effective way. The air coming up from beneath is

A camp grate with a separate under grid. This may serve as the support for a charcoal fire.

a great help. While upon the subject, I might add that a small package of charcoal poked away in the car does not come amiss at times.

In another United outfit is found a further development of the camp grate. This is the addition of a folding wind shield. The main intent of this shield is to retain the heat so that one can cook faster. Likewise, when the master of ceremonies stands either at the back or end of the fire, he is protected from its direct heat. When using one of these shields it is a wise plan to dig out a small hole under the lower edge of the back for a draft.

When the wind blows especially hard, a wind shield becomes almost a necessity, both from the

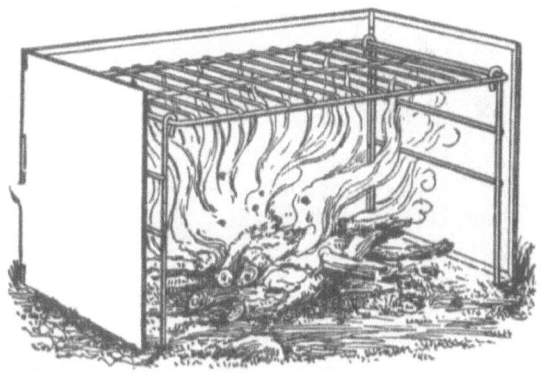

A folding wind shield added to a camp grate. This retains the heat and one can cook faster.

standpoint of retaining heat and the danger of spreading fire. You may be interested to know that you have an emergency wind shield with you in the form of the engine hood. In any case, whenever it is windy, a fire should be built in a trench or depression and always on the lee side of the car and tent; also, some distance away so that there is no danger from flying sparks.

The camp grate becomes even more resourceful in the case of the Red-E folding broiler, stove, and oven. The grate and wind shield part are along the general lines of the United outfit but in addition there is a baking and roasting oven attached to the back of the shield. The top of the back is hinged in such a way that it can be

The oven when detached from the folding broiler, stove, and oven is to all intents a reflector baker.

opened to inspect the baking. When the oven is not used for this purpose it can serve as a place in which to keep dishes and food warm. The complete Red-E outfit when folded is 18 inches long, 10 inches wide, and only 1½ inches thick. In using any of these grate outfits it is advisable that it should be confined in a canvas carrying case when not in use. Otherwise, everything it comes in contact with will get smudged. Likewise, it would not be out of order to handle one with a pair of cotton gloves.

A combined drawing and photo designed to show the construction of the tentobed. (See Chapter X.)

A broiler, stove, and oven which is only 1½ inches thick when folded.

The oven attachment of the Red-E outfit is to all intents a reflector baker, and the baker is an article of such ancient and honorable lineage that at least it deserves passing comment. As a matter of fact, the good housewives in Revolutionary times baked their biscuits before hearth fires with reflecting bakers of much the same sort that are used in camping for the purpose to-day.

The reflector baker which you can buy in any outfitting store may be aluminum, tinned steel, or iron. The front of this article is open and the top slants back like the shed of a roof, while the bottom slants up to meet it. Inside the baker is a flat shelf which holds the food. The open front is placed facing the fire. The heat reflected from below, on top, and the sides, insures even baking. An aluminum baker of this sort weighs next to nothing and is not more than a half inch thick when folded.

Harking back to the wind shield used in connection with a grate, the idea, as I have said, is to retain all possible heat for cooking. Some motor campers who will have none of compromise, carry this idea to its ultimate conclusion and lug along a whole wood stove, chimney and all. Undeniably, a stove holds the most heat and it is a simple enough matter to get a folding wood stove which is so compact and light in weight that it is no special inconvenience while traveling.

In the type of folding stove most practicable for motor camping the bottom and one end are open. The fire, of course, is built on the ground. The Scott stove is a good outfit of this sort. It weighs only 7½ pounds and when folded, even with the chimney, is only three quarters of an inch thick. When set up it is 9 inches high, 13 inches wide, and 2 feet long. The Burch Klunk Unit stove is another of the same sort which folds very compactly.

Of course, the motor camper needs to be sure that he is really going to use a wood stove. In many parts of the West, carrying a wood stove would be akin to carting coals to Newcastle. Many of the cities and some of the National parks and forests provide ready built stoves or fireplaces for the camper. In Chapter XVI I will give further details upon this subject.

CHAPTER VII

FOOD BOXES

Glass Jars—An Ingenious Home-Made Box—Fresh Food Versus Canned—Another Running-Board Box—Refrigerators—The Tin Food Box—Folding Outfits—Food Containers

STRICTLY "according to Hoyle," glass containers or fragile ware of any sort have no place in a camping trip. When food bags, friction top tins, or paraffined cardboard containers can be used to good advantage it is wise to give one or all of these the preference over glass. At the same time, experience tells me that one of the handiest and most satisfactory food containers in the world, provided it can be carried conveniently and doesn't break, is either the Mason or the lightning sealing glass jar—preferably the latter.

Both quart and pint glass jars are used quite extensively in motor camping and so far as I have observed the breakage mortality rate seems astonishingly low. Of course, much depends upon the roads one travels and the care with which the jars are packed. As a rule, each jar should be carried in a separate, loose-fitting bag. These, in turn, may be packed in a food case.

One time in Spokane I ran across a motor camper who had a very neat and orderly sheet metal running-board food box. Most of the food supply was contained in glass jars. He told me that he had planned and built the outfit himself during winter evenings. He was as proud of it as a hen with a brood of new chicks. Certainly, the outfit showed considerable ingenuity and exceptionally good workmanship.

I will describe this food box for it may give you some pointers worth using. It was stationed on the left running board; the depth was that of the running board, it was as high as the top of the tonneau door, and the width extended from the rear end of the running board to the front seat door. The left-side tonneau door was permanently closed while traveling but both front seat doors were free.

The front and back of the box were each large single sheets of galvanized iron. Top, bottom, sides, and back were solidly riveted together, but the whole front sheet was detachable. While on the road, this was held in place by bolts but in

A home devised sheet metal, running-board food box. This is described in the text. The camper is filling his gasoline stove.

FOOD BOXES

camp it was taken off and with the addition of two steel rods for support, became a good dining table. The box was secured to the running board by bolts through the bottom of the box and further braced higher up by a rod attachment to the side of the car. There was not one chance in a million of that food box breaking loose.

All around the inside edges were glued strips of felt padding so that with the front firmly bolted in place there remained slight chance for dust to trickle through. This was a wise precaution. The owner told me that before adding this felt he had been unable to keep dust out but since then there had been no trouble at all. The interior of the box contained two shelves holding foodstuffs, mostly in jars. Between the jars were small wood partitions which prevented them from rubbing against each other. These partitions were loose and detachable so that if one wished to rearrange the jars, this could be readily done. In the lower space under the second shelf were packed a gasoline stove and the cooking utensils. The entire exterior of the box was painted a black enamel and was very neat in appearance.

In some respects, this home-made device is the best motor camping food box I have ever seen. It is rain and dust proof, securely attached, the culinary department is largely a single unit, and there is practically no unpacking to be done, for the box itself is a camp cupboard with all food neatly arranged in a row. On the other hand, there is a considerable amount of space allotted to canned and bottled stuff—more I think than the average motor camper finds necessary.

As regards food, it has been my experience that some motor campers load up with provisions as though they were setting out for an expedition to the heart of Darkest Africa. Some even haul such a load half-way across the continent. I think this is a mistake. Fresh food is best when one can get it and considering the numerous towns through which one passes and the many farmers in between there is slight reason for the camping party to find lack thereof.

Wholesome food and regular meals are important. Fresh eggs, milk, and vegetables from the farms, fresh meat from the butcher, and perchance fresh fish from the wayside lakes and streams are advantages which should be grasped. Perhaps in no other type of camping trip is one so constantly in close touch with fresh markets. Of course, at all times one needs to carry staple foods such as coffee, tea, sugar, and so on, and there should always be on hand a twenty-four hour emergency supply of canned stuff. In touring through parts of the Southwest or in crossing the desert it is advisable to double this emergency supply. It is wise to be prepared for breakdowns.

In this matter of fresh foods, perhaps I do not give sufficient consideration to parties that drive off into the byways and camp for days or weeks in the wilderness. In some of the National forests of the West, for example, motor camping parties sometimes have a way of cutting themselves entirely adrift from ordinary sources of food supply for weeks at a time. Of course, in such instances the necessity for carrying a bountiful food supply is self-evident. If it suits the fancy of a camper to run off on a side ramble of this sort he can always stock up accordingly at the right time and place.

Coming back to running-board boxes, another well-constructed home-devised outfit I have run across is well worth describing. The machine which carried this was a large touring car and the passenger list a rather sizable one. The right running board carried beds, folding chairs, and two or three other pieces of equipment. A huge double tent of the lean-to variety fitted on the rear. The left running board accommodated the box in question.

The specifications of this particular box are as

follows: It is 50 inches long, thus extending practically the full length of the running board and 26 inches high. The bottom is 12 inches wide while the top is only 9 inches wide. In general appearance, the outfit when closed reminds one of an upright piano box. Various suit-case trunks used in motoring are of the same general lines and very likely one of these was the inspiration for the idea.

The front is in two lengthwise sections, one hinged to the top of the box and the other to the bottom so that in opening one flanges down and the other up. The box is made of three-ply basswood and the addition of a covering all around of enameled duck keeps out dust and rain. The interior is partitioned into two main compartments, the larger of these being as high as the box and thirty-three inches long. In this, snugly fits a large sized suit case containing clothing and other personal effects. Packed above the suit case is an air mattress.

The remaining seventeen inches of lengthwise space in the box is devoted to culinary matters. This is subdivided into five smaller compartments. In the upper left-hand corner is packed a coffee pot, bacon, and ham. The one next to it holds six one pound boxes of coffee, sugar, flour, meal, rolled oats, and rice. In the left middle compart-

Upper photo shows a well-constructed, home-devised, running-board box. It is described in detail in the text.

Lower photo: an insulated refrigerator basket for carrying perishable food.

FOOD BOXES

ment are canned goods of various sorts—milk, soups, Crisco, and so on. The right middle space is given over to a fifty-one piece set of nested aluminum ware such as I have described in Chapter V. In the lower compartment next to the running board fits a two-burner gasoline stove.

This box while touring is permanently fastened to the running board with two bolts at each end. Of course, the two left-side doors of the car are always blocked. With this equipment, the owner and his family covered more than six thousand miles during one summer and fall.

I have seen dozens of home-devised running-board boxes and so far as I can recall no two of these have been exactly alike. The fact that each has appeared to fulfill its duty to the eminent satisfaction of the persons immediately concerned makes it rather difficult to define just what constitutes the best outfit. In many respects, the home-made box, properly constructed, proves more satisfactory than a manufactured article.

In any outfit, due provision should be made for perishable food. One sees quite a few small running-board refrigerators in use among motor campers. Many of these are of home construction; perhaps a tin cake box with a drain tube soldered on near the bottom, or a wood box of the same sort lined with zinc. I have even heard of a discarded fireless cooker doing service as a running-board ice chest. In Chapter IV I have mentioned the cooling possibilities of a water bag when the top is one of open construction; a bottle of milk or jar of butter can be set in the water and kept perfectly cool.

There are numerous manufactured ice boxes designed to fit the running board. An outfit of this sort is usually about 10 inches wide, and ranges from 26 to 36 inches in length. There is one of totally different construction from this type known as the Burlington refrigerator basket which I like rather better. This can be carried either on the running board or in the tonneau. It is somewhat unusual in appearance in that it looks like an ordinary rattan basket.

The outer covering of this outfit is woven reed and beneath this are several layers of insulating material. These are what keep in the cold. Inside the layers is a metal lining divided into two compartments, one for ice and the other for food. The ice compartment is much the smaller of the two and it is removable. When the ice melts this is taken out and the water poured off. The lid, also lined with metal and detachable, breaks

FOOD BOXES

on hinges in the middle so that it is a simple matter to get into either end of the basket.

The life of a cake of ice in an insulated box of this sort is probably longer than in the home-made variety of refrigerator. As to whether or not an ice box is a necessity during a motor-camping trip is another question. In my humble opinion, it is a nice thing to have along if there is plenty of room for it but I would hardly class it as a necessity.

So far as keeping perishable food fresh is concerned, an ordinary tin cake or bread box lined throughout with corrugated paper usually serves well enough. This has some disadvantages in that meat and certain other foods should not be left in tin for any length of time, but jars of butter, milk, and similar foods will keep in good condition. Meat can be carried in limited quantity in a small bag or wood box inside the car, away from the heat of the sun.

The tin food box can perhaps be carried to best advantage on the running board. It should have a water- and dust-proof covering of some material such as pantasote and it is important that this fit rather loosely so that air will circulate freely between the cover and the box. A good way to hold it in place is by means of two metal loops screwed into the running board, one at each end of the box. Then a strap is run over the top connecting these. If the sun beats down terrifically hard on the box while traveling, it is just as well to carry it inside the car for the time being. Such a box properly packed will usually hold a good part of both the perishable and staple food supply.

In regard to food boxes in general, there are two outfits which are unique. Neither of these is especially suitable for carrying perishable foods. They are better adapted for canned stuff, utensils, and other articles. The unique feature is that each is a combination carrier and dining table. One of these is the Stoll suit-case table. When folded it has much the appearance of an ordinary suit case except that along the edges are metal strips and the opening is across the center of one side.

This outfit measures $6\frac{1}{2}$ by 18 by 24 inches over all and when empty weighs 18 pounds. The moment it is opened for use, the suit case appearance quickly vanishes. At each end are slots in which are nested telescoping legs and these slide down and become the supports of a table. Presently, the two doors which form the suit-case cover are turned back and you have the two end leaves of the table top in place. In between are

The whimsical, hungry porcupine. Keep food so he will not get at it.
Courtesy of All Outdoors.

FOOD BOXES

two more folding leaves which go to make up the rest of the table top. Beneath these are the contents of the case.

The other outfit of the same combined feature is the Dyas folding cupboard. This is ten pounds heavier than the Stoll outfit and is of somewhat different construction. A feature which may be of special advantage in camp is built-in screening on the sides. There is also an extra shelf which fits over the top. When set up the main table measures 3 feet by 2 feet by 9 inches. The folded size is 9 by 12 by 36 inches.

By way of a few odd suggestions concerning food containers, I might say that paper cartons once they have been opened become a nuisance. The flapjack flour for example, if carried in its original package, leaks and gets over everything. Best to dump it immediately into a jar.

Never allow canned provisions to remain in the tins after they have been opened or poisoning may result. Canned milk will keep for a certain time in its tin after being opened but the usual method of stopping up the two small openings at the top with whittled slivers of wood hardly prevents it from spilling. A surer way is that of sticking two small squares of adhesive tape over the holes.

Be sure that the containers in which coffee and

tea are carried are air tight. Otherwise, the beans and leaves will lose their flavor. The best way to carry butter is either in a glass jar or paraffined cardboard cup. Cardboard containers of various sizes (not the thin paper kind) will be found useful in many ways.

Whenever you turn in for the night, remember the birds that fly, animals that walk, insects that crawl, and chipmunks that do all three. See that your food is thief proof. It is wise to hang it from the limb of a tree when this is possible. So far as meat is concerned, the meat safe which I have described in Chapter V is good protection. Beware especially of the chattering little chipmunk and the roly-poly porcupine. They won't leave anything but crumbs behind if they have their way.

CHAPTER VIII

THE NIGHT'S SLEEP

Variable Temperatures—Blankets—Sleeping Bags—Comforters—Bough Beds—Folding Canvas Cots—Cot Overhead Frame-Work—Cotton "Slabs"—The Kapok Mattress—The Air Mattress

IN any kind of camping trip, whether afoot, by canoe, or motor car, sleeping equipment is in many respects the most important item of all. Perhaps the camper's greatest need is a comfortable night's sleep. If this is lost or seriously disturbed, he is completely used up. Be sure not to overlook the importance of this; especially as the sleeping equipment problem can be solved more easily in motor camping than in most other kinds of outdoor trips. Not every outdoors man is so fortunately situated that during the daytime he can completely forget the existence of his bed. If walking, the husky, pulling pack on his back is a constant reminder.

The sole purpose of bedding equipment is bodily comfort. If a camper is firmly convinced that he cannot receive bodily comfort with anything short of a four-poster bed, I am almost inclined to think that it might be worth his while to take one along. The fact remains that bedding comfort in motor camping is possible with very much less. In no way need this matter be taken to extremes. Equip yourself according to your needs with a weather eye on weight and convenience and you will find that comfort can be wrapped in a surprisingly small bundle.

In figuring out the necessary amount of bedding, bear in mind that night temperature is a variable quantity. You can go camping in New York with a reasonable amount of assurance that the summer nights will be fairly mild. In Maine, they are somewhat colder. On identically the same nights in the high Rockies, the thermometer is likely to hit freezing. The motorist making a cross-continent trip must have bedding equipment to meet all manner of conditions.

Bedding, beds, and shelter are so closely linked together in some of the motor camping outfits that it is not altogether easy to discuss each separately. However, so far as possible I will confine the present chapter to bedding and beds and in the following two chapters take up car beds and combination beds and tents.

THE NIGHT'S SLEEP

Irrespective of the sort of bed one sleeps upon, blankets or sleeping bags are of prime necessity. Many of us who have followed outdoor matters to some extent are sharply divided upon the question of which of these two coverings is the most satisfactory. I must admit that I am somewhat neutral in the matter although as I review my past experience, this seems to show a slight leaning toward sleeping bags. Both are good and I think that so far as motor camping is concerned, "both" is the wise solution. I would have one sleeping bag apiece and a suitable reserve supply of blankets to draw upon as needed. As a matter of fact, blankets alone will serve, for one of these can be sewed or pinned into the form of a sleeping bag merely by stitching up the foot and side or by the use of blanket pins (include a number of blanket pins in your equipment).

Use only wool blankets. Those of cotton are worse than useless in camping. Furthermore, several light weight wool blankets are preferable to one heavy blanket of the same total weight. The reason for this lies in the insulation afforded by the air chambers between the layers. The same rule applies to sleeping bags. I take it more or less for granted that you do not crave white sheets and pillow cases while camping. To be sure, such luxury is wholly possible and it is practiced by some motor campers but I think most people will find that the extra bother hardly pays. This luxury is reasonably practicable when a camping trailer is used; an outfit which is described in Chapter XII.

In regard to the discussion of blankets versus sleeping bags when each is used separately, it may be said that there is a knack about rolling up in a blanket so that you will not wake up in the middle of the night and find most of it off you. Even when blankets are laid flat on a bed, the cold shivers sometimes creep down one's neck. This is especially true if the sleeper is inclined to be a bit restless. With the sleeping bag, on the other hand, you are tied in so that you can't roll out. Also, a sleeping bag obviates the cold neck chills by means of special flaps which can be drawn around the head. This is not always true of a home-made bag unless special strips are sewed to the top.

There are several good manufactured sleeping bags which can be bought at any outfitting store. The salesman will probably tell you that you need a waterproof canvas cover such as goes with most of these bags, but I think this doubtful. I will describe a bag in my own outfit of which I think

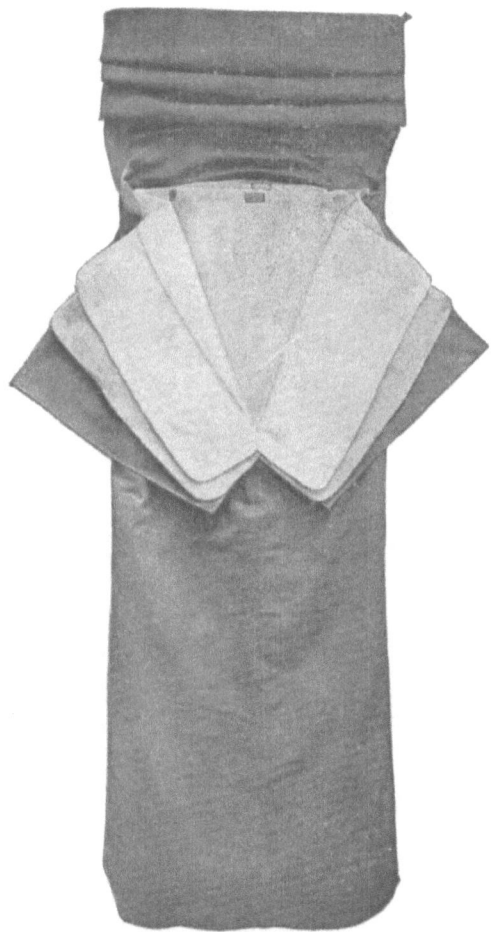

Layers of light weight sleeping bags confined within a canvas cover. More bags can be added when necessary.

THE NIGHT'S SLEEP

very highly. This is known as the Kenwood. The quality of the wool is excellent, the bag is easily carried and light enough in weight to be adaptable to various weather conditions. It is made in such a way that if you wish to add more bags, these can be nested one inside the other in much the manner of a nested cooking utensil outfit. If the weather is moderate, a single bag is sufficient covering; on colder nights, one or two more bags can be added. I think, however, that blankets instead of additional bags is about as simple an arrangement. That is the way I use the outfit. The top of the bag is equipped with special flaps which form a double thickness of wool. This offers ample protection around the neck and shoulders. The Kenwood concern also makes an outdoor rug, which is convertible into bag shape. I have never used it but it looks quite practicable.

The ordinary, soft, cushiony bed comforter when used as a covering is, in a way, a contradiction to what I have said concerning insulation in that here you have one heavy covering instead of several light ones. The fact remains, that the comforter makes a good covering and always a fine mattress, especially so if filled with wool. The comforter like a blanket can be sewed into the form of a sleeping bag if you wish. Anyone fortunate enough to own a heavy eiderdown comforter is especially well fixed. The cotton comforter is not so suitable. In any case, it is advisable to enclose the comforter in a covering of light washable material or else it will get frightfully soiled.

I own a sleeping bag known as the Downisilk which to all intents is a comforter sewed into bag form, except that the covering is soft mercerized khaki and the material inside is wholly different. This filling is kapok, more commonly known as "silk floss." This material is somewhat similar to cotton in appearance but it is neither silk nor cotton. It is a vegetable fiber of silky-like texture which grows in the seed pods of the randoe tree in the island of Java. Because of its unusual lightness and buoyancy it is used to a considerable extent in life preserver boat cushions. Its use in sleeping bags is something of an innovation although mattresses have been made from this material for some time.

This kapok bag is exceptionally warm and soft. I have derived a good deal of comfort from it on sundry cold nights but on the other hand there is not the flexibility to it that is true of several blanket coverings. You have warmth even when you do not wish it. At all times, however, it can

Ordinarily, bough beds are laid upon the ground. This shows one of especially elaborate construction above the ground. Weaving ropes back and forth hold up the boughs.

be used as a mattress and it makes a mighty good one. It weighs only six pounds, but like a comforter has the disadvantage of being bulky.

I will now take up beds and mattresses. Going to the other extreme from the chap who can't be happy in anything less than a four-poster bed we occasionally find a hobo minded motor-camper who favors the primitive method of rolling up in blankets on the bare ground. The red-blooded hero in the movies may commit such indiscretions by preference and some of the rest of us are forced to once and awhile by necessity but my surest word of advice would be, "don't do it."

A good bough bed or mattress on the ground, even a canvas sheet, is a wholly different matter. Sleeping without such under protection has the twofold disadvantage of being hard on the health and mighty hard on the bones of your body.

The next bed that presents itself may be the one of pine boughs gathered in the woods. This is more like. Here you have insulation between body and ground and a bed which if thick enough and properly built is to my mind one of the most soothing and comfortable mattresses in the world. The aroma alone from the fragrant needles is warranted to put to sleep the most veritable victim of insomnia. It is the very breath of the woods. The bough bed, however, is hardly dependable enough for the average motor camping trip. In the first place, the boughs are not always available and in the second place, even when they are, it takes time to cut and lay them.

There are many different types of waterproof sleeping bags designed to be used without tent shelter. An occasional motor camper uses one of these but he is the exception. Most outfits of this sort are more suitable for other kinds of camping. The average motor camper, wisely enough, sleeps either under canvas or under the car roof.

The folding canvas cot is used very extensively in motor camping. There are many good points in its favor. For one thing, you are sleeping high and dry above the ground; for another, when the cot is not being used as a bed it makes a convenient settee and when not needed at all can easily be folded up and poked away to make room for plenty of living space in the tent. The folding cot is fairly light in weight, clean, easy to air, and makes a bundle that fits comfortably in most any car.

The size of the standard army cot when set up is 6 feet 6 inches long, 27 inches wide, and 16¾ inches high. It folds to 5 inches by 8 inches by 3 feet 3 inches long. The weight is 21 pounds.

The standard army cot both set up and folded for carrying.

A steel-stay type of cot. Swivel joints make it adjustable to uneven ground.

The double width cot. A dividing rail runs down the center.

A single cot with mosquito netting framework attached.

THE NIGHT'S SLEEP

This is the cot which seems to be used most. It is built for hard service and will stand plenty of it. There are two other single cots, however, designed to give more comfort. One of these is the Gold Medal wide cot. It is of the same general construction as the army cot and weighs about the same but it is 36 inches wide. There is a distinct advantage in this additional width. Anyone who has experienced the chilly draughts which creep in around the edges of a narrow cot will appreciate this fact.

The other bed is the Gold Medal automatic cot. This is of narrow width. The particular variety of discomfort which this cot aims to overcome is uneven ground. Steel stays, running from one leg to the next in a somewhat crisscross fashion and connected by swivel joints adjust the cot to uneven surfaces so you always lie straight. The outfit is the same width and length as the army cot, but weighs only 16 pounds. Also, it folds to a package only 32 inches long.

Do not make the mistake of thinking of the wide cot which I have described in terms of a possible double bed. An easy way of inviting misery is for two people to sleep on one folding cot. As a rule, one person to each cot. There is a permissible exception to this, however, in the case of the

Gold Medal really and truly double width cot. This is an outfit which is especially built to accommodate two people. In this outfit there is a dividing rail in the center of the cot and running its full length. There are two quite separate beds in one. The complete outfit folds into one fairly compact bundle.

The people that make these cots have discovered further possibilities. They have found that the addition of a few sticks of framework here and there play strange magic. For example, a mosquito frame consisting of uprights and cross bars draped with netting and attached to the head and foot of a cot will make you immune from these whining pests. They also have a tent framework which fits over both single and double cots in much the same fashion. There is even a tent extension frame which may be added to the double cot frame thus giving living room as well as bed shelter after canvas has been draped over it. A complete framework of this sort weighs 30 pounds and folds to 5 feet by 5 inches in diameter. The Gold Medal concern manufactures only the cots and framework, not the tent to fit them. This is supposed to be made by a local tent maker.

You may know from experience that sleeping on bare canvas without any under covering sometimes

The evolution of a double cot. Upper photo shows overhead framework to which can be added canvas for sleeping shelter alone. Center photo: an extension frame added for living quarters. Lower: canvas over complete frame.

bears a striking resemblance to lying on a cake of ice. You need fully as much bedding under as over you—twice as much is better still. A standard size blanket doubled over just about covers the canvas surface of a single cot and under average conditions may be mattress enough. A motor-car robe is good; also a bed comforter. A few newspapers laid on the canvas often prove effective in repelling chilly draughts.

A comfortable enough mattress, I presume, so far as softness is concerned is one aptly known in the West as a "slab." This has about the thickness of a comforter, it is cut to the exact width and length of the cot, and filled with cotton padding. These cotton slabs seem to be well liked by motor campers. As to whether or not they are really effective in repulsing cold and dampness is an open question. My prejudice against cotton in camp is so strong that I have never tried one.

Infinitely superior, to my mind, are small kapok mattresses of somewhat the same sort. Furthermore, these weigh less and cost very little more. With a kapok mattress underneath, one can even sleep on the ground, without any serious results.

In some respects, the most comfortable and

luxuriant outdoor bed upon which one can sleep is an air mattress. Some time ago I received a letter from a camper who had been experimenting with sleeping on the ground and later had come around to using a bed of this kind. The letter is so aptly related to some of the discussion in this chapter that I cannot resist the temptation to give it in part. Speaking of his first camping experience the writer says:

"We read all the books obtainable and decided to try our luck. The first night out we struck a snag. We waited until it was too late, and the result was that we could not get suitable material to make our bough bed.

"What happened? We were turning and tossing all night trying to locate a soft spot or find a hole to put our hip and shoulder bones in. When we got up in the morning we were tired and sore and aching in all bones in our bodies. Just think of trying to sleep on a bucking horse's back. Unless you have the sticking qualities of a caterpillar, you will roll off and get your bumps.

"This was rehearsed many times until we came across the air mattress—which was more air than mattress. I can tell you, this was a whole lot better than playing hide-and-seek with the hard spots in a bough bed, stones, and other hard spots

An outdoor rug convertible
into bag shape.

A kapok mattress and pillow.

on the ground, not to mention the dampness and other effects."

I think the bough beds upon which the writer of this letter slept must have been crudely built ones; there is something of a knack in building a good bough bed. Nevertheless, I can readily understand the satisfaction which he derives from an air mattress. It is literally true, that with a billowy mattress of this sort, one can sleep with perfect comfort either on top of a pile of sharp rocks or on damp, swampy ground.

The air mattress is an accommodating piece of equipment; more so than most other kinds of mattresses. Its respective hardness or softness is entirely dependent upon how much air you blow into it. When inflated, it is a somewhat formidable package, but with the air out, it shrinks into a small, easily carried bundle. Air mattresses are made in various widths ranging from 25 to 54 inches. The lengths vary from 45 to 75 inches. The shorter length mattresses are hardly as satisfactory as those of full length but may do well enough when used on a cot. They are long enough to rest the body from the shoulders to below the hips. As a usual thing, there is no abrupt drop for the legs; the mattress tapers down gradually.

As to whether or not the camper, headed in the direction of cold nights, will find the air mattress wholly suitable is something of an open question. I have heard it accused of harboring cold air when the thermometer shoots down toward freezing. I have never slept upon one at such times so cannot say from experience how much there is in this. It is a point worth considering. In any case, you are sleeping above the damp ground, so I see no reason why warm blanket layers between the body and the rubber should not fortify one against the cold.

In the following two chapters I will take up numerous other types of beds, some of which are quite radically different from any of those so far mentioned.

CHAPTER IX

SLEEPING IN THE CAR

The Sawed Down Back—Seat Cushions as Mattress—The Mid-Air Suspended Canvas Mat—The Car Cot—Car Versus Tent Shelter

MOTOR camping beds are extremely varied. An air mattress convert may be enjoying a comfortable sleep *on* air, close to the ground, while the next camper, perhaps equally comfortable is suspended *in* air, four or five feet above him. The latter, I make haste to add, is sleeping upon a type of equipment commonly known as the "car bed." There are several ingenious devices whereby the interior of the car is utilized as a sleeping compartment, thus in many cases doing away with the necessity for a tent.

Sleeping quarters of this sort are not possible in all types of cars. A tonneau, as found in the five or seven passenger touring car is essential. They may sometimes be possible with a limousine or sedan but a touring car is best. Even so, sleeping accommodations are distinctly limited, unless extra facilities are carried. There is not room in the car for more than two sleepers although now and then a youngster can curl up in an extra nook.

Sometimes, the car owner turns carpenter and builds his own car bed. I have seen a number of this kind which seemed to answer very well. The idea is one warranted to strike a responsive chord in both the imaginative and practical strain of most any motorist. In instances where this idea is actually put into practice, it usually seems to take the form of sawing down the back of the front seat so that after hinges have been attached, this can be dropped down to form a bed. During driving hours, the back is held up by hook attachments.

Not every car owner is especially keen about wielding hammer, saw, and chisel in the somewhat promiscuous manner which such an arrangement necessitates. He may harbor the vision of selling the car some day at a fairly good price, and in such cases it is doubtful if the prospective buyer will look upon the sawed down seat in the light of an improvement.

Other home built car beds one sees upon the road are canvas stretcher arrangements about as wide

SLEEPING IN THE CAR

and nearly as long as the interior of the car. Such an outfit is suspended mid-air (although supported from below) above the tops of the front and rear seats. Most of these seem to be patterned from a similar type of manufactured outfit which I will presently describe. First, however, I will tell of a manufactured device which gives much the same result as the sawed down front seat but which obviates any tinkering upon the construction of the car.

In this outfit, known as the McMillin bed, seat cushions do service as a mattress. This is accomplished by means of adjustable steel rods which run from the top of the front seat to that of the rear, the ends of the rods conforming to the arcs of the backs. The procedure of making up this bed is quick and simple. The seat cushions are removed from the car and then the steel rods are laid in place after the manner mentioned. The cushions are gathered up again and placed side by side upon the supporting rods. On this foundation and extending over the top of the front seat is stretched a large canvas sheet. The two front corners of this are roped to the wind shield and the rear corners to the side brackets. You sleep upon the canvas with the cushions underneath serving as a mattress.

Seat cushions and tonneau space are variable quantities, of course, but the rods which hold the cushions are adjustable and this permits of considerable leeway. These rods will fit most any touring car. Exceptions to this rule are the Ford and Chevrolet cars. The construction of these two machines is such that the cushions are too wide to drop between the front and back seat so a slightly differently constructed bed is used. In all cases, the bed is wide and long enough to accommodate two people. The complete frame and cover weighs sixteen pounds and folds into a compact bundle.

In the majority of instances, the manufactured car bed is a sizable stretcher of tightly drawn canvas so that you are literally sleeping in mid-air. It differs from the ordinary stretcher in that the two rails are at head and foot, instead of along the sides. There is no under mattress. Fairly typical of this type of outfit is the Des Moines bed. This is a large piece of heavy khaki with wood cross pieces at each end. These are supported by legs, front and rear. The outfit is anchored to the respective ends of the car on both sides by ropes and straps. The amount of rigidity or sag to the canvas bed depends upon the strap adjustment.

A suspended canvas car bed. The tension device is designed to eliminate sagging. Small photo shows the bed rolled up like an umbrella, and one means of carrying it.

Courtesy of *Outing*

The main difference between several beds of this sort is the construction of either the back or front supports. I do not think that there is sufficient variation to make any essential difference. The Genessee bed is of the same general construction as the Des Moines but differs in that at one end a few short heavy steel springs are inserted in the canvas. This is designed to give the bed more flexibility. In the ABC bed, another outfit, there is a special device designed to prevent the bed from sagging to the middle.

Of course, in any outfit of this kind, the greatest amount of width and length conveniently possible, is desirable. Especially good length is found in the Des Moines and ABC beds. I might add that all beds of this type are in no sense hammocks, in spite of the fact that they are suspended in air above the car seats. The main source of support is from below. This difference is quite basic so far as comfort is concerned. A bed of this kind weighs only about twelve pounds, and when not in use rolls up quite compactly on one of its cross bars.

The construction of this type of bed is quite different from that of the ordinary folding cot in that no side rails are used. There is another kind of car bed, however, which more closely resembles a folding cot in this one respect although it is different in several other particulars. The framework is of one half inch galvanized tubing to which is attached on both sides and ends the canvas sleeping surface. This outfit is known by the trade name, Peoria Auto Kot. It is six feet long and 2 feet wide. Two of these cots will fit side by side in any five or seven passenger touring car, with the exception of the Ford. A special size is made for Fords.

On each cross piece of the tubing frame of this outfit, both front and rear, are two rest supports, these in the shape of an inverted letter U. All four of these fit over the top curve of the upholstery of the respective front and back seats. The canvas is stretched just tight enough to allow it to sag a bit for the sake of comfort but not enough to touch the rests underneath. The framework of the outfit is hinged crosswise in the middle so that when not in use it folds over making a package three feet long and two feet wide. The most convenient place to carry it as a usual thing is in the tonneau, snugly against the back of the front seat.

Coming to a general discussion of the car-bed method of going motor camping, I find much to commend it. With the side curtains in place, you are as snugly fortified against wind and rain as in

Two of these cots are laid side by side in a touring car. The framework is galvanized tubing. The cot folds to half its length.

Courtesy of *Outing*

most tents. On cold mornings, by letting the motor run a few minutes you will have the warmth of a steam-heated apartment. You are sleeping high above the dampness and crawling things of the ground. There is room to store baggage under the bed so that all belongings, as well, are safe and sound under one roof. Motorists who use these car beds seem to find them uncommonly comfortable (plenty of under covering must be used).

On the other hand, one is likely to feel cramped for room, at the best—especially so, in rainy weather. This car-sleeping method with the total elimination of tents is used a great deal and with eminent satisfaction. So far as I personally am concerned, if it came to an out and out alternative between sleeping in a tent and sleeping in the car, I would choose the tent. Yet I am duly impressed with the value of the car method under certain conditions. Like the auxilary power in a drifting yacht, it is often a mighty convenient thing to have along. It sometimes serves as a valuable adjunct to a camping trip. Say, that a man and his wife in planning a motor camping trip are partial to a small tent, but this doesn't exactly seem to fit into the sphere of things because a friend is going along as well. A car bed together with the tent may solve the problem.

CHAPTER X

COMBINATION BEDS AND TENTS

One Man Bed and Shelter—The Two Classes of Canvas Beds—Why Lengthwise Bed Tension is Most Comfortable for Two People—The Lean-to Shelter— A One-legged Bed—Steel Beds and Spring Mattresses—How a Running-Board Bed is Packed— A Feather Bed

NUMEROUS outfits used in motor camping are combination beds and tents. In some cases, these are set up apart from the car, in others, attached to the side of the car, and there are a number of outfits which can be set up either way. In practically all cases, the bed is the important feature of an outfit of this sort. With some few exceptions, the tent part is designed only to serve as a shelter for the bed. There is little or no room in the tent for living space.

Perhaps the most extreme instance of this fact is found in an outfit known as the Tent Cot. The basis of this is a four-legged wood bed frame somewhat after the lines of an ordinary folding canvas cot except that it has real springs instead of canvas. Attached to the side and end bed rails is a mite of a bow framed tent which resembles something between an old time prairie schooner and a baby carriage top. The lower edges of this small tent are permanently attached to the bed rails. This shelter is nothing more than a hood, but it is high and wide enough for one to crawl under and sleep secure from rain and wind. There is a large opening at each side and in addition to these there are windows at both ends. Any of these openings can easily be closed tight. The bed is very comfortable but it must be remembered that one is lying over diamond-shaped indentations of wire springs, so a mattress of some sort is essential. A light weight kopak mattress answers very well.

This tent cot, of course, is set up apart from the car. The single size cot is $6\frac{1}{2}$ feet long and 28 inches wide. This folds to the same width, and 3 feet 3 inches long. It weighs 23 pounds. A double cot of the same construction is 44 inches wide and weighs 32 pounds.

A man traveling alone derives a good deal of comfort from this little outfit. It can be set up in a moment without any bother, and so far as it goes, gives perfect shelter. It is not always so easy to carry as some other outfits in that there are either twenty-eight or forty-four inches of width to contend with; however, this depends almost entirely upon individual packing arrangements. Usually, the most convenient way to carry it is on edge upon the running board so that the bed fits snugly against the side of the car.

In this outfit, no ropes, poles, or stakes are necessary. The same is true of another combination outfit called the Tentobed. In this case, however, there is more head room and the tent reaches all the way to the ground, thus giving a certain amount of storage space underneath. Like the other outfit, the tent part merely serves as a shelter for the bed, although if two of these outfits are carried, a canopy can be raised between them. There are neither springs nor mattress in this outfit. The sleeping surface is a sheet of twelve ounce duck. This is provided with a tension regulating device which takes up the stretch. The bed is very comfortable.

There are two different sizes of the Tentobed outfit; in one, the bed is 4 feet 6 inches wide and 6 feet 4 inches long while in the other it is the same length but six inches narrower. In each case, the outfit when packed measures 4 feet 6 inches by 7 inches in diameter. The respective

Upper photo: this is to show the relative size of the tent cot. Center: the outfit set up. Lower: one method of carrying it when folded.

COMBINATION BEDS AND TENTS 113

weights are fifty and forty-five pounds. Comparing the Tent Cot and Tentobed in a general way, I think the former will often be found the most comfortable outfit for one person and the latter the more suitable for two.

The ordinary canvas folding cot with the addition of overhead framework and canvas becomes much the same type of combination tent and bed as the two outfits just described. In Chapter VIII I have mentioned such possibilities. The double cot is rather more suitable than the narrow width cot in this respect. A completely equipped and comfortable outfit of this sort, including cots, tent, mattress, and cover is the Wilson Roll-A-Bed tent. The tent, however, is confined solely to the cots; there is no extension frame-work for a living room such as has been mentioned in Chapter VIII.

The various canvas beds used in motor camping may be said to fall into two general classes; those in which the greater amount of surface tension is crosswise, and those in which the greater amount is lengthwise. The ordinary folding canvas cot is the best example of the former, the side rails being the obvious reason. That is why a bed of the general army cot type, unless it has a dividing rail down the center, is unsuitable for the use of more than one person, irrespective of how wide it may be; two occupants will roll together in the center.

The class of canvas bed without side rails is more comfortable for two people sleeping on one stretch of canvas. Most of the suspended car beds mentioned in Chapter IX are of this general type. It is also found in a number of outfits which are combination tents and beds.

In some respects, the most unique example of head to foot tension without the presence of side rails is found in the ABC combination bed and tent. This outfit is attached to the side of the car. The style of tent used is one found very extensively in motor camping; the front of the tent faces the side of the car and the car top does service as a ridge pole. The tent is of the general lean-to type with which every woodsman has long been familiar. The roof slopes down from the car top in shed-like fashion.

The bed which this tent shelters is a canvas mat with head and foot rails but no side rails of any kind. The head is supported by clamps attached to the running board and which hold the head rail in place, a few inches above the board. Oddly enough, the remaining support consists of a single leg directly under the center of the mat. The

Showing the process of setting up the roll-a-bed tent.

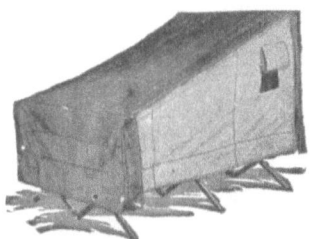

The same outfit all set up and proof against rain.

More air by raising one side. Mosquito proof by adding netting.

The roll-a-bed tent outfit including a hair mattress packed on the running board.

upper end of this leg is attached to the head rail from which it runs down in a diagonal direction to the ground. Halfway down, are a number of notches and in one of these fits a stretcher bar attached to the foot rail. The bed can be raised

A unique running-board combination bed and tent. Note the one-legged feature.

or lowered by changing the positions of the bar in these notches. This bed will support great weight and is not drawn out of center, even with two or three people sitting on one side.

The standard size double bed of this outfit is 54 inches wide, 80 inches long and it weighs 20 pounds. The single bed is the same length and 30 inches wide. The weight of tents vary according to size and material. A balloon cloth tent (which is excellent) makes the complete double outfit weigh thirty-five pounds. This folds into a compact package which is readily strapped to the running board.

There are number of camping variations possible with this, and several other outfits which I describe in the present and following chapters. For example, very often the car does double ridge pole duty; two outfits are taken along, one for either side of the car. On the other hand, it is convenient now and then to set up tents apart from the car. This calls for the use of tent poles. If there is only one tent, the front flap may be raised so that it forms a canopy. If there are two tents, these can be set up facing each other some distance apart and the two raised front flaps joined, thus affording outdoor living quarters underneath.

Varied arrangements of this sort are possible with the Burch canvas bed and tent. This bed differs from the ABC outfit in that there are side rails, although these are not connected in any way to the sides of the canvas bed mat. The strain is wholly from head to foot rails. Attached to the bed frame is a rachet for stretching the canvas when this begins to sag a bit. The bed may be set up independently both of car and tent; there are no running board attachments. The type of tent with which it is usually used is the lean-to, attached to the car top, although this is

COMBINATION BEDS AND TENTS 117

by no means necessary as it can be set up in most any kind of tent. A combination outfit comprising this canvas bed and a 5 by 7 foot lean-to tent weighs 43 pounds.

All these motor camping beds are so surprisingly comfortable that comparison, from the standpoint of comfort, is extremely difficult; so I take refuge in description. I will now describe a unique type of folding combination outfit which has steel beds and spring mattresses. Such a piece of equipment does not weigh more than sixty-five pounds all told and when not in use fits so compactly upon the running board that neither front nor rear doors are blocked in any way. I will try to give a more or less composite picture of two outfits of this sort, one known as the Schilling, and the other as the Stoll.

The tent is the shed roof, lean-to type, attached to the side of the car, using the car top as a ridge pole. The bed frame consists of several steel parts which when unfolded and assembled give the outfit the general appearance of any good metal bed covered by a canopy. In standard size outfits the tent is only as long and wide as the bed—there is no extra room inside. The end wall of the tent is held up by a stretcher bar attached to the bed side rails and extending above these.

The head rail of the bed is bolted to the running board. Along the length of this rail are attached a row of twenty-odd small coil springs. A similar row of springs are attached to the foot rail. Each of these respective head and foot springs are connected by a small cable running the length of the bed. In the Schilling outfit, this connection consists of a series of small flat links, while in the Stoll it is a strong wire. In both cases, these many connections are permanently enclosed in canvas fabric, so that you have a perfectly smooth surface to sleep upon. The tension is wholly from head to foot and from about every standpoint you have a mighty comfortable bed. As in the case of canvas cots, however, plenty of extra under covering is needed during cold nights. The term "mattress" as applied to this particular type of bed does not refer to a thick, soft pad. It means simply the combination of springs and canvas mat.

Of course, the construction of the respective Schilling and Stoll outfits differ in details but both are so well made that perhaps these differences can hardly be called essential. The Schilling bed measures 48 inches wide by 78 inches long and the complete outfit with tent and cover weighs 65 pounds; the Stoll bed measures 46 inches by 75 inches and the complete outfit weighs 63 pounds.

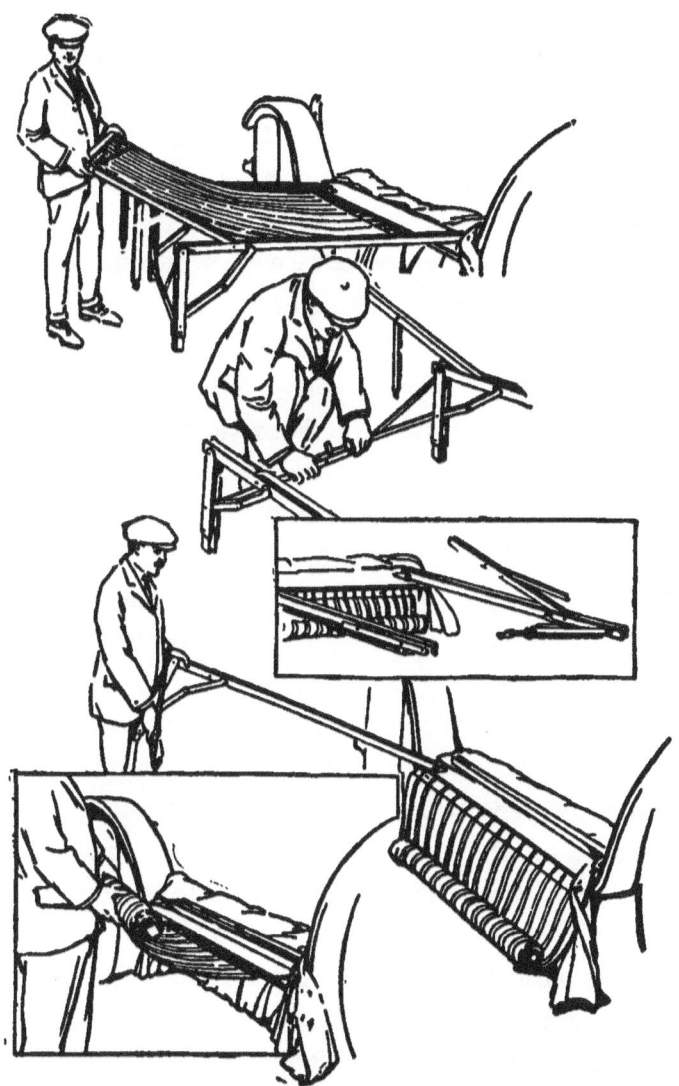

The various operations in taking down and folding the Schilling type of steel bed after the tent has been removed.

If one is keen about a tent that can readily be set up apart from the car perhaps the Stoll is the easier of the two to operate. On the other hand, the running-board attachment of the Schilling outfit while traveling strikes me as being the most secure.

In order to show the ease with which an outfit of this sort can be taken down and folded for traveling, I will describe the operation of the Schilling. The process either of setting up or taking down requires only from three to five minutes. First, the tent is taken down and folded, then the bed tackled. The tension of the mattress is loosened by lifting up the foot bar. The mattress is rolled up upon the foot bar, as one would wind up a roll of cloth. Cross stays of the bed frame are unlatched and these together with the legs and folding parts of the side rails nest compactly within the respective side rails. Each rail with its nested parts is swung around into a position, side by side on the running board and the mattress roll is laid over these. The tent and a cover are added. That is all there is to it.

This outfit will fit most any car made that has a top. Both long and short running boards can be accommodated, although sometimes slight adjustments have to be made when the running board

The small package on the running board is the Schilling model of combination bed and tent.

How the same running-board outfit looks when unpacked and set up. The tent is drawn aside to show the construction of the bed.

All fixed for the night.

COMBINATION BEDS AND TENTS 121

is especially short. Such difficulties are usually overcome easily but it is best to find out about them beforehand. Short running boards having some of the older types of straight fenders are not so easy to fit. When closed cars are used, small metal straps are furnished for the tent attachment above.

A quite differently constructed outfit from the Stoll and Schilling and one not quite so compact but more versatile, is the Anderson collapsible tent and bed. The tent in this case is of the same general lean-to type but is set up apart from the car. The bed has a steel frame, and the springs somewhat resemble those on your bed at home except that they roll up. And, if you please, a feather mattress is laid over these. The bed alone weighs 53 pounds. It is 6 feet 2 inches long, 4 feet wide, and 18 inches high. When rolled up, it is 4 feet long and 7 inches in diameter. The additional tent weight varies according to circumstances.

In this outfit, the bed itself, instead of the car, supports the tent. The general principle is the same as that of the cot overhead frame, mentioned in the first part of this chapter but the result in some respects is more satisfactory. The reason for this is that the overhead supporting rails, connected at the head and foot of the bed, flange out and forward, away from the bed instead of vertically or inward as in the case of the cots. Hence, the upper ends of these rails represent the peak of the tent and the result is more space inside.

The Anderson type of bed both set up and folded.

Further room is available by raising the front flap of the tent so that it forms a roof parallel to the ground. If one wishes, ringed wall curtains can then be added to the three sides.

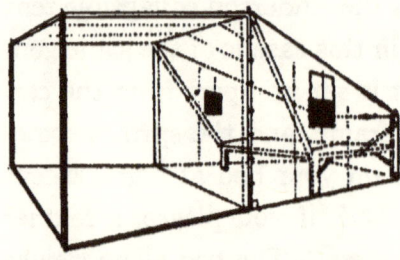

How the bed serves as a foundation for tent support. This arrangement is shown by photo on another page.

Another variation is an arrangement whereby the front flap becomes one side of a wedge tent. Small additions are made to the flap and then the lower edge is pegged to the ground. There is not so much head room as with the wall curtain arrangement. About the most comfortable tent of all is had by the addition of a second bed and proportionate amount of canvas. This variation gives a roomy wall tent 6 feet 6 inches by 14 feet.

The Anderson combination bed and tent. More living space by raising front flap and adding wall curtains.

How this outfit looks when carried on the running board of a car.

A variation of this tent by adding more canvas to the front flap and pegging it to the ground.

COMBINATION BEDS AND TENTS

Regarding as a general type, the various outfits described in this chapter, it may be said that each of these is, to a relative degree, a ready made solution of both the bed and tent problem in motor camping equipment. Taken as a whole, the chief limitation of these outfits is tent space. I am

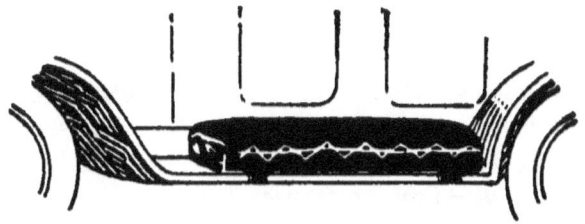

The Stoll type of combination bed and tent packed on the running board.

speaking specifically of standard size equipment (there is no general standard; each manufacturer has his own pet standard size). In several of these combinations such as the ABC, Burch, and Stoll, it is quite possible and sometimes advisable to use a larger size tent in connection with the bed, provided the car is one which has facilities for supporting it. This usually means a touring or similar style of car with a long roof. As against this, the standard size outfit is suitable both for a runabout and touring car.

CHAPTER XI

MOTOR CAMPING TENTS

Car Supported Tents—Single and Double Tents—Shelter for the Car—The Sewed-in Floor—Wall, Marquee, Wedge, and Miner Tents—Color and Material—Tent Accessories

CONSIDERING shelter alone, to the exclusion of beds and all else, it may be said that a great many tents used in motor camping are of the same lean-to construction found in the combination beds and tents but usually larger. The necessity of lugging ridge and tent poles along is obviated, for the top of the car does service in this respect. To all intents, and sometimes actually, this tent, considered as shelter alone, is one of the combination outfits previously described with the bed part left out. The camper solves his own bed problem by carrying cots along or in whatever way seems best.

As a rule the length of the ridge in a tent of this sort should be the same as that of the car top.

MOTOR CAMPING TENTS

A tent that fits a Ford perfectly would make a Packard look like a sixteen-year-old boy trying to squeeze into the short pants he wore when he was six. Get the size that fits your car. The absence of tent poles is comforting but at the same time there are places where the presence of these might prove to be a distinct convenience. One is likely to run off on short day trips now and then leaving the tent and rest of the camp equipment behind. Poles can be cut or either jointed poles or telescoping rods carried. Most car-supported tents can be pitched apart from the car, with the addition of poles.

A lean-to shelter tent on only one side of the car is usually called a single tent. There is a considerable amount of variety to these single tents. In some instances the ridge is supported either by straps fastened to the bows of the car or by ropes thrown over the car top and anchored on the opposite side. Several simple outfits of this sort such as the Strong and the Genesee are quite inexpensive and may often serve well enough.

There are a number of other outfits which through the more liberal use of canvas are designed to give varying degrees of shelter to the car and greater privacy and shelter to the campers. This is true to a limited extent of the Burch single tent. In this case, the top of the tent extends across the car top and well down the other side. Thus, the interior of the car is well sheltered on both sides and can be used both as a dressing and store room. This car shelter idea is carried further in both a Baker-Lockwood and in a Scott tent. In these instances the canvas reaches all the way to the ground so that only the front part of the car beyond the dash is exposed. In both the Des Moines single tent and the Burch Ideal tent there are no reservations—everything and everybody is under canvas. Such complete shelter practically amounts to having along a portable garage.

As a final step in the versatile and somewhat profligate use of canvas as practiced by motor camping outfitters, we find the double tent. This is two single tents, one on each side of the car with a connecting canvas cover running across the top of the car. In the Burch double outfit, the car is mostly under cover and can be made entirely so by the addition of slip-on covers. One of these covers fits over the hood and front wheels and the other on the rear end. Varying degrees of car shelter are found in the Athol, the Strong, and other double outfits.

In the Des Moines double tent the shelter is so complete that a passerby might walk by without

The Burch single tent of the lean-to type set up apart from the car.

Camping with a trailer of the four-wheel trailer car model. (See Chapter XII.)

realizing that a touring car was housed underneath. Many campers find distinct advantages in such complete privacy and shelter; at least, one can tinker with the engine on rainy days without getting wet. The Des Moines double outfit such

Slip-on Covers. These may be used to advantage in conjunction with a tent that shelters the car body.

as is used with a large touring car represents a huge stretch of canvas yet this weighs only thirty-four pounds. The camping space underneath is approximately seven feet out from the sides of the car and the length is as great as is required to cover the car, this varying with different models. The size used with the Ford weighs something less than twenty-five pounds.

A feature found in some lean-to tents which I do not altogether admire is the sewed-in floor. This is supposed to be a great advantage and as proof of this fact you are allowed to pay something extra for it—although in most cases it will be left out entirely if you but say the word.

In a tent which is used solely for sleeping purposes, I have no particular objection to the sewed-in canvas floor; it has distinct advantages. A tent that is being lived in both day and night is another matter. You are sure to track in dirt. Likewise, oil and gasoline are about, and on rainy days you will probably cook inside the tent. The floor being a part of the tent makes things rather messy at the best.

A canvas floor is desirable but one which is detachable and can be taken out and cleaned now and then is likely to prove more satisfactory. This, in connection with a sod cloth gives a tent which proves most effective against draughts, insects, and dampness. A sod cloth is a strip of canvas about nine or ten inches wide sewed to the bottom of the tent on the inside. It is held down by stones or similar weights.

In all the tents so far mentioned which make use of car attachments for support, the front faces the side of the car. There is only one tent so far as I know, of which the reverse is true. For this reason if no other, it is worthy of mention, but also, it has one point which will appeal quite strongly to some campers. You can build your

Complete shelter for car and campers. Upper photo: the Des Moines single tent. Lower: the double tent.

camp fire out front and sit in the tent facing it. This tent, the Abercrombie, is more of the wedge style than lean-to. The back guys of the tent are tied to the car. Perhaps the main disadvan-

With a shelter of this type you can build the camp fire out front and sit in the tent facing it.

tage of this arrangement is that you sacrifice the use of the car as a dressing room.

The majority of outfits described in the present and foregoing chapter are expressly designed for the motor camper and they are used almost exclusively by him. Of course, the lean-to style of tent is not new but its special construction for adaptation to the motor car is wholly so. There are numerous other styles of tents which were in use long before the motor car appeared upon the scene. Some of these are used quite extensively to-day by motor campers.

Everybody knows the Wall tent. All things considered, this is perhaps the most comfortable tent in existence. It is a shelter, however, which can hardly be called the most suitable for campers more or less on the go; there is too much bother and fuss about setting up and taking it down. Yet, in spite of this it is quite a favorite with motor campers. I think, however, that unless you plan to camp for a long time in one place you will find that the labor involved in handling a wall tent hardly compensates for its roomy comfort.

The main source of bother with a wall tent has always been the ridge pole. Recently, a "poleless" wall tent has appeared. Only the two end uprights are needed and each of these is made in three sections for folding. The ridge pole substitute consists of two leverage arrangements above each upright. Although a tent of this sort can hardly be expected to set as well as one with a solid ridge pole, it is at the same time probably more suitable for the motor camper who is intent upon having a wall tent.

Another well-known tent and one which has

Motor camping in a Wyoming National Forest. At the left is shown a Miner tent set up with the jointed poles on the outside. The shelter at the extreme right is a well-pitched Wall tent.

Motor camping with a Marquee tent. The front flap can be attached to the car top thus giving an outdoor living-room.

recently taken on a new lease of life because of its popularity with motor campers is the marquee tent. This is not surprising for it is an outfit which is expecially suitable for the purpose. It is light in weight, simple to erect, and exceptionally comfortable for two people. By attaching the front flap to the car top one has an outdoor living room between the tent and side of the car. One tent pole inside is all that is needed to hold this tent up.

One of these tents having ground dimensions of 8 by 8 feet is 8½ feet high. Such a generous amount of head room is quite exceptional for any kind of tent. The back wall has a large window and in front is a detachable door with a mosquito-proof window. When the front of the tent is being used as a living room, the door can be detached and set up either side of the raised front flap and thus do service as a wind shield.

The wedge tent is another shelter which is light and easy to pitch although it has not the head room of the marquee. The wedge tent can be set up either with or without poles. If there are plenty of trees about, its ridge may be suspended by a rope strung between two of these. If there is only one tree, the car top can be the other. If no trees at all, the car top can still take care of one end of the ridge and an upright pole with guys running out front, the other.

This shows how the car top may serve as a pole for the wedge tent.

A tent long in use on the western plains but not so well known in the East is the miner. This is a pyramidal tent of the same general ground proportions as the marquee but with not such good head room possibilities. I must admit to a strong personal liking for the miner tent, mainly because of its ability on sundry occasions to shed rain easily and stand up safely under a good sized gale. The sharp pitch of the roof is responsible for this. Likewise, it accounts for the popularity of this tent upon the plains.

There are three different ways in which a miner tent can be set up. One of these is by means of a single upright pole inside the tent, after the manner of the marquee. Another is to attach the peak to the overhanging limb of a tree. The third is that of using two poles outside like the legs of a tripod. Because of the limited amount of head room in the tent there are certain advantages in the two outside methods of rigging it. Jointed poles are often carried.

To paraphrase Robert Louis Stevenson, "there are such a number of tents in the world that I'm sure we should be as happy as kings." There are a dozen and one tents in existence other than I have mentioned. I think, however, that I have covered the ground rather completely so far as those most suitable for motor camping are concerned. The reason for the existence of such a gay and varied galaxy of tents is that such a thing as a perfect tent does not exist. No one tent has everything that a tent should have. The best one can hope for is a compromise which comes the closest to filling one's particular needs.

The particular compromise which one camper finds suitable may be wholly different from that of another. I think that you will agree with me, however, when I say that the possibilities of comfortable bed and shelter are sufficiently varied and numerous to meet most comers. Provided a given outfit does not seem exactly to fill the bill, you may find it worth while to review the present and three foregoing chapters with a view to suitable combinations. In one case, this may mean a single lean-to tent with attached bed, combined with a car sleeping arrangement; in another, possibly, two single lean-to tents, one with bed

Two single lean-to tents of the Stoll type, one with bed attached and the other to serve as a living room. (See Chapter X.)

attached and the other to serve as a living room—in this case, extra canvas cots can be carried and folded and put out of the way during the daytime. There are many possible combinations of this sort. In all cases, however, one must carefully figure out weight and packing adaptability. One outfit may chime in with another perfectly while a third may not fit into the sphere of things at all.

Coming back for the moment to tents; as regards

The combination of the three outfits shown on this page may give comfortable accommodations for a fair-sized motor camping party. Upper photo: the two single lean-to tents set up facing each other apart from the car.

Lower photo: a car bed. Occupants of this can take advantage of outdoor living-room shown above.

MOTOR CAMPING TENTS

color, olive, khaki, or even green, are each a more comfortable color than white. Standard army khaki duck will shed water better than white duck. The former is the best grade of duck; many of the tents I have described are made of this fabric, although in some cases one has a choice in the matter as regards material. An excellent, although more costly, alternative when one wishes to save weight is a cloth variously known as "balloon silk," "silkette," and other trade names. This is a very finely woven cotton fabric which weighs only about three and one half ounces to the yard. As against this, most duck used in motor camping tents weighs eight or ten ounces to the yard.

For tent windows and tent front, in order to fool the mosquitoes, the best material is bobbinet. This is a more expensive name for mosquito netting. It is well worth the difference, however, so far as results are concerned. Practically all window tents come ready equipped with bobbinet.

In folding a tent, pay as much attention to its natural creases as you would to those of your own trousers. Do not sling it together in any old way. Make a careful study of just how it is folded when you receive it from the manufacturer. A tent should always be carried in a separate bag so that it is out of harm's way from being torn or cluttered with dust and dirt. Either a heavy canvas bag or one of oilcloth with the glazed side in does very well.

If tent poles are carried, these should be of proper length and jointed. Some of the combination tent and bed outfits make use of a telescopic rod of tubing; the lower end is driven into the ground. In selecting a wood pole, make sure that it is straight grained and preferably of some hard wood such as ash or maple. A standard size tent pole which is both light and sturdy is the government shelter tent pole. This when folded is fifteen inches long and opens out to forty-four inches.

Seemingly of minor importance but a detail which sometimes assumes large proportions in camping is the matter of pegs. Wood pegs cut along the way will answer well enough but I think that light weight steel pegs are better. They save time, labor, and, oftentimes, temper.

CHAPTER XII

THE CAMPING TRAILER

Principle of Operation—Combined Carry-all and Portable Canvas Home—Various Models—Two Versus Four Wheel Trailer—The Motor Bungalow—Importance of the Hitch—Backing around Corners

THE motor camping trailer is more or less in a class by itself. Much that I have said concerning beds, tents, and packing applies to the trailer only to a relative degree, if at all. The trailer is a ready-made solution of all three. So, if everyone went motor camping in this particular way, there would be few problems left to discuss. Instead of this, we find that there is no outfit used in motor camping about which there is such great difference of opinion as there is about the trailer.

One man will tell you that this is the only way in the world to go camping. He is so enthusiastic about his trailer that he will hardly tolerate any criticism of it. Another man is likely to qualify his praise. He will admit that the trailer is a mighty comfortable home in camp but he may add that he has found it something of a nuisance at times while traveling.

The trailer, considered as a type, is an unpowered vehicle weighing between five hundred and eight hundred pounds which is towed behind the motor car while on the road. It is an up-to-date pack mule for it carries the complete camp equipment—tent, beds, stove, cooking kit, ice box, food, camp furniture, and personal baggage. An additional load of five or six hundred pounds above its own weight is a quite common occurrence. Sometimes the trailer even carts along a canoe, duck boat, or similar small craft.

Considering the trailer solely as a carry-all, its advantages are obvious. The camping equipment just doesn't exist, so far as the car is concerned; you have the freedom of a clear deck. And freedom of this sort while touring is a thing not to be scorned. With some people, it is the most important element of all.

Provided the trailer is a workable proposition (which it is) it would seem at first thought that my reiterated suggestions in this book to figure carefully on weight in motor camping were somewhat misplaced. In many respects, the trailer method of camping undeniably is "going heavy." At the

Off to the woods with a trailer. The car is free of all equipment; the trailer is an up-to-date pack mule. This party is taking along a sectional rowboat in addition to the regular camp outfit.

THE CAMPING TRAILER 139

same time, the towing burden is not so great as may appear upon the surface. I will explain.

The basic ideas involved in car burden and trailer burden are quite different. In one case, the load is being carried while in the other it is pulled. A horse can drag a load which he could not hold on his back. By the same token, it would be foolhardy to place the weight of a trailer load on a motor car body. Yet, when this same weight is towed behind, the car pulls it along easily and safely at a speed of between twenty and thirty miles an hour. The power is in the car and the trailer makes use of it, although of course a certain amount of additional power is necessary. Taking an average trailer fully equipped for the road, it has been figured that the additional power required in the motor car is something less than one half the extra power that would be needed to carry an equal load in the car itself.

There are a number of different types of trailers. Some of these have slight reference to motor camping. Farmers use them a great deal for hauling milk, provisions, and cattle to market. A trailer of this sort usually consists of a wood wagon box which is supported by either two or four wheels, as the case may be. In front is a draw pole which is hitched to the rear of the motor car. Trailers of this sort, while not intended primarily for camping, are sometimes used for this purpose. In parts of the West, I have seen these doing seven-day-a-week service—five and one half for business, and one and a half for recreation.

A trailer of this sort is solely a carry-all, irrespective of whether this means farm products or camping equipment. On the other hand, the type of trailer which is especially built for motor camping is considerably more than a carry-all. It is a comfortable summer home on wheels.

The basic construction of this camping trailer is the same as that of the farmer's outfit—a low wood box supported in some cases by two wheels, in others, four. Sometimes solid rubber tires are used but as a rule the wheels are equipped with pneumatics. These cost more but their cushioning qualities are worth the difference. Trailer tires wear about twice as long as those on the car itself. The main reason for this is that they are not subject to the strain from the driving mechanism of the car.

The height of this camping trailer when fully equipped and packed for the road varies with different makes. In the Auto-Kamp outfit, for example, the height is hardly greater than that of the trailer box, with the result that this small

THE CAMPING TRAILER   141

towed vehicle is not especially conspicuous—in no case can the trailer be called strictly inconspicuous. In another model, the top is about on a level with that of the car top, and others are of varying heights. In all cases, the contents are securely covered either by canvas or enamel drill so that dust or rain will not get inside.

Upon stripping off the cover you find quite a surprise box before your eyes. When ready to make camp, the trailer itself becomes your home. It is bedroom, dining room, and kitchen all in one; practically a portable house, ready for light housekeeping. Figuratively speaking, you press a button and the trailer becomes a tent house three times as wide as its width when acting as a carry-all. Two comfortable beds with steel springs and thick mattresses open and fall easily into place; these beds are built in as part of the trailer. When opened, each flanges over one of the wheels, several feet above the ground. Each bed is wide enough to accommodate two sleepers. A sheet draped from the ridge of the tent gives two separate bedrooms.

Covering the complete outfit is a tent supported by a folding framework which is part of the trailer. In all cases this tent is of the general wall tent type although the nature of the roof varies with different makes. In the Auto-Kamp, the Kampercar, the Curtis, and one or two other models there is a peak, similar to that of any wall tent; in the Hesse trailer, and the Lyons trailer, the roof is flat, like that of a motor car top. The head room, that is, height from trailer floor to top of tent, varies in these different makes from six to six and one half feet.

The standard equipment in addition to tent and frame which goes with a trailer is about as follows, although there are some slight variations: two double wire spring beds and mattresses, collapsible table, collapsible shelves, food box, ice box, and folding gasoline stove. These, and any additional articles of equipment, are packed in such a manner that they are easily obtainable but not in the way. In one or two instances the ice box and food box are attached to the under side of the trailer floor and are pulled out like the drawers of a desk.

The floor space of the trailer between the beds serves as a living room. There is plenty of space for a table and the edges of the two beds serve as seats. In fair weather, one naturally chooses the outdoors as a dining room but when rain comes the trailer interior makes a very pleasant canvas home.

The method of folding the beds for traveling is

A trailer model of especially compact construction. This unpowered vehicle carries the complete camp equipment.

The beds and framework of the above trailer unfolded for camping.

With canvas added, the trailer becomes bedroom, dining-room, and kitchen all in one. This shows the two-wheel Auto-Kamp model.

a point about which there is a divergence in various models. The height of the trailer when equipped for the road is dependent upon this element. The beds of the Auto-Kamp outfit, for example, fold completely over so that the two nest together and are parallel to the floor. There is sufficient space left between the floor and the folded beds above to accommodate a fair amount of equipment. The intent of this arrangement is compactness.

In both the Curtis and Hesse trailers, on the other hand, the beds do not come into contact with each other at all. Instead of this, they are tipped up straight on edge and thus form two walls. The purpose in this case is to leave available a large amount of space for packing equipment. In the Curtis outfit, this space is forty-four inches high and forty-four inches wide. The height in the Hesse is not so great as each bed breaks on hinges in the center. As to whether the compact, or the roomy arrangement is best, depends upon what the motor camper wants and needs most.

No two makes of camping trailers are alike any more than two motor cars are the same. In about a half dozen different kinds, however, tire sizes are pretty well standardized throughout. The universal size is 30 by 3 inches. In all cases but one the standard 1¼ inch ball bearing axle is used (a plain bearing axle would be wholly unsuitable). Some trailers have two wheels and others four.

A mooted question in trailer discussion is the so-called superiority of four wheels over two. In theory, at any rate, the four wheeler has several advantages. It is claimed that this type of outfit carries its own load without putting a considerable amount of strain upon the car in front; that it does away with all whipping motion (to some extent inevitable in the two wheeler); that it cuts the bumps in two while going over rough roads and follows a car around corners more easily than two wheel trailers.

The advocate of the two wheeler replies that two additional wheels are in themselves just so much additional weight; that they represent just so much greater initial and maintenance expense and even if there is some slight advantage (which he will not admit), this is not sufficient to warrant the additional weight and cost.

The matter remains something of an open question with no decision rendered. Two wheelers seem to be the ones used most. An outfit of this sort ready for the road with standard equipment (not extras) weighs between six and seven hundred pounds. The Auto-Kamp and the Curtis are examples of this type. A four wheeler, such as the Hesse and the Trailercar, equipped in the same way, run a trifle over eight hundred pounds.

The general type of trailer which I have described is the sort which the average motorist buys when he wants a trailer and is willing to pay the price. Such an outfit is costly but not exhorbitant. It is not to be confused with the expensive and luxuriant "land yachts" which the newspapers tell about now and then. These in spite of their luxury are, as a rule, not nearly such workable outfits as the ordinary camping trailer. A two thousand pound palace car is likely to come to grief when wallowing through a bad mudhole.

An outfit which possibly might be classed as being of the general "palace car" type but very much lighter in weight and hence more practicable than others is the Adams Motor Bungalo. The weight in this case is not greater than that of some of the trailers which I have described. It is considerably more luxuriant and by the same token costs about three times as much. The principle of operation is much the same except that the top is permanently raised and there are lockers, clothes presses, and a number of similar conveniences. The original Bungalo was invented by Glenn H. Curtiss, the airplane maker, for his personal use but this was rather large for general use. The one being made now is a smaller model after the same design.

Regarding trailers as a whole; at the beginning of this chapter I mentioned the praise and condemnation of the trailer as expressed by users. This divergence of opinion is not difficult to understand. If a trailer is what a man wants, and provided it runs true to form, he can entirely dismiss from his mind camping equipment while on the road, and at any time in from five to seven minutes after stopping, he can enjoy the comforts of a summer cottage.

Much of the criticism of the trailer has been due to the fact that it sometimes fails to run true to form while on the road. I think that much of this concerns the past rather than present. For several years, trailers were in an experimental stage. A number of firms quit making them entirely. Those which persisted have been making steady improvements with the result that the trailer is much more of an established working proposition that it was a few years ago.

In some cases, a trailer will drag, whip, bump, or refuse to track perfectly. In nine times out of ten, the troublemaker is the hitch by which it is fastened to the car. The average man buying a

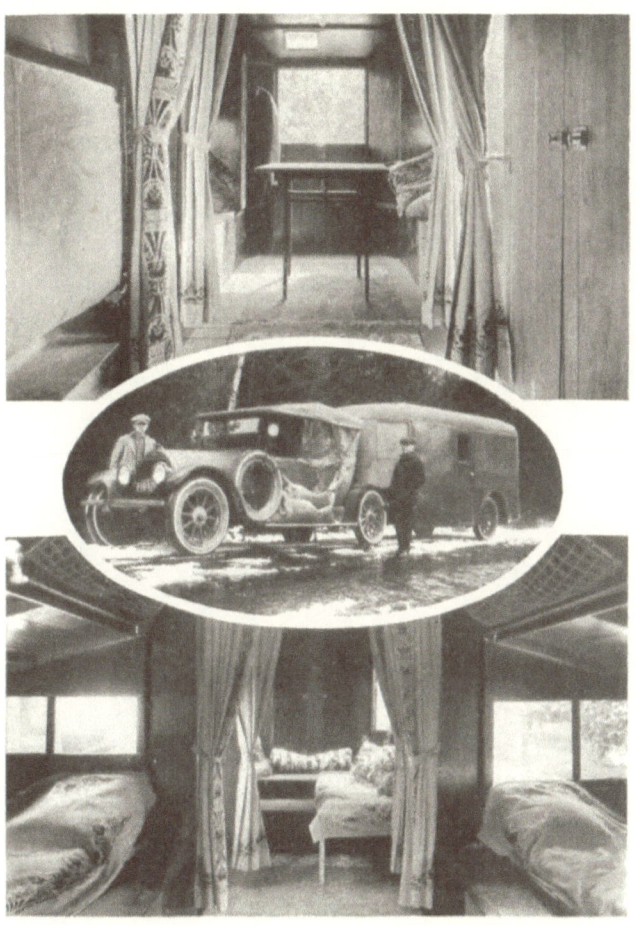

The elaborate trailer home invented by Glenn H. Curtiss, the airplane maker, for his personal use. Upper photo is an aft view of the interior showing lockers, table, and clothes presses. Lower photo: forward view showing sleeping accommodations. The model manufactured for general use is smaller than this.

THE CAMPING TRAILER 147

trailer is likely to overlook this detail but it is an all important one. There is no hitch which without certain adjustments is equally suitable for all kinds of motor cars. The great variance in motor-car construction is the reason for this. Each hitch must be fitted individually to a given car. Insist upon this. If the hitch is properly attached, the trailer probably will ride along with comparative ease.

Considering the fact that the trailer is an independent car, its conduct on the road is surprisingly laudable. Even at the best, however, the trailer can never be wholly a part of the car. Very often it will have its little jokes at your expense; but some of these are easily forestalled after you become accustomed to its ways. For example, most trailers have a profound distaste for backing around corners.

An accompanying drawing shows the way a motorist ordinarily turns the front wheels when he wishes to back around a corner. It also shows the course which the trailer wheels are likely to take with such a start; this is far from being the desired result. Another drawing shows how the start should really be made when a trailer is attached to the rear. In this case, the car wheels are started in the wrong direction but those of the trailer are headed in the right direction. With this situation, the front wheels are quickly thrown

Left drawing shows the usual start in backing around a corner, and the way the trailer will go. Center and right drawing show the proper procedure.

around so that the car backs correctly and now that the trailer wheels are started right, they will continue so.

CHAPTER XIII

CAMP FURNISHINGS

Tables and Chairs—Folding Camp Cupboard—Wall Pocket—Clothes Hangers—Lantern—Medicine Kit —Personal Equipment List

TAKING camping as a whole, the luxury of tables and chairs is only for those who camp permanently in one spot. Campers who are more or less continually on the go hardly find it convenient to carry along camp furniture. But there are exceptions to every rule and perhaps the most notable exception to this old time edict is modern motor camping. Very few motor camping parties entirely scorn the use of tables and chairs.

A picnic on the grass during a single day's outing is a pleasant little custom. Three meals a day, however, day in and day out so close to Mother Earth is another matter. The comfort of sitting on a chair of some sort and having one's meals served on a real dining table is a little refinement of society that is more satisfactory for steady diet.

It isn't absolutely essential but it is very pleasant. On the other hand, this thing may easily be taken to extremes. I have seen motor camping parties loaded up with almost enough camp furniture to fill a seven-room house. Such a load represents a good deal of comfort during camping hours but it is likely to give rise to considerable discomfort while on the road.

Of course the car itself offers certain possibilities in the way of tables and chairs. The running board on occasion serves as a seat; the car cushions when placed on the ground have the disadvantage of being rather low but on the other hand they are mighty soft; the engine hood when inverted may sometimes make a passable table. These and similar points are worth looking into but as a rule they hardly go far enough in themselves. Combine a little ingenuity with one or two of these and you may have a really workable scheme.

For example, it is possible to devise folding leg arrangements which can be attached to the under sides of the car cushions and thus make them the same height above the ground which they are above the floor of the car. As a matter of fact, one manufacturer years ago figured this thing out and presently produced an outfit known as the Burch Pullman Chair. This is an excellent device

CAMP FURNISHINGS 151

and is used somewhat extensively in motor camping. It consists of a folding steel frame upon which is placed one of the seat cushions. Two of these frames, one for each cushion, nest within each other and when not in use are carried in the tonneau under the back cushion. Thus packed, they raise the seat only about three quarters of an inch.

The folding army cot is a potential settee, perhaps a table. A better auxiliary canvas table,

A running-board canvas bed minus its tent doing auxiliary service as a table.

however, is one in which there is an absence of any sagging. The ABC canvas bed, for example, described in Chapter X is more on a level and when the tent is removed makes an excellent table.

Motor campers who remain for a considerable length of time in one place often manage to dig up stray pieces of packing boxes and from these pound together acceptable enough tables, benches, and a cupboard or two. Under the circumstances, perhaps this is as good a way as any. This method, however, hardly goes far when one is continually on the move. Provided due wisdom is used concerning weight and packing ability, I think that a certain amount of folding camp furniture is a wise investment for the average motor camper.

There are many different kinds of folding tables, some of quite unusual construction. As an example of this fact I might point out the two combination tables and food carriers which I have described in Chapter VII. In all instances, the folding table, like the folding cot, is a piece of collapsible furniture which when not in use doubles up like a contortionist. The weight of such outfits vary all the way from about five to twenty pounds. Generally speaking, the heavier ones are stronger and more rigid. There are times, however, when a light weight table may prove more suitable.

A most substantial and rigid outfit is the Gold Medal folding camp table. The size of the top is 27 by 36 inches and it is 28 inches above the ground. When folded, the top encloses the legs so

A motorist in the motor camping grounds in Banff, Canada, plans a month's stay and furnishes his camp to suit.

that the outfit is 3 feet long by 5 inches by 7 inches. It weighs 19 pounds. An added convenience that may go with this outfit is a folding shelf made separately from the table but which can be fitted between the legs half way between the ground and the top. The shelf adds five pounds to the weight. This table and shelf outfit is fine for a permanent camp but the weight is against it for any camper steadily on the go.

Another Gold Medal outfit of the same size but of different construction and several pounds lighter in weight is the roll-top table. An unusual feature of this outfit is that if you wish, you can buy the roll top minus the legs. You cut and plant your own table legs in camp. Four crotched saplings of equal height as legs and two more for cross-pieces becomes the table support. This arrangement saves a certain amount of weight and bulk while on the road.

The same idea of furnishing your own legs is found in a somewhat smaller and very much lighter Abercrombie and Fitch outfit. Indeed, this is the lightest table top which I know about. It weighs only three pounds. The top consists of a row of wood slats inserted in a pantasote covering, A set of folding legs can be carried in addition if one wishes but these add considerably to the weight.

Really a more practicable A. and F. outfit is the telescope table. The top in this case is permanently attached to the frame, but the outfit rolls up into a fairly compact bundle. It weighs about twelve pounds.

Another interesting departure is the Stoll outing table (a different outfit from the suit-case table). The top consists of a row of two and one half inch wood panels woven together. The under frame is steel and of a construction which reminds one of two open umbrellas with their points placed end to end. The outfit is quite automatic and can be set up or collapsed very quickly. When folded it is 30 inches long and 5½ inches in diameter. The weight is 8 pounds.

Of wholly different construction is the Polhamus Colapso stand, although this also has steel legs. A sectional steel frame likewise borders the entire top. Due to this sectional feature, the length of the top is adjustable from 32 to 40 inches. It is 2 feet wide and 2 feet high. The whole outfit when folded fits into a package 2 feet long by 6 inches in diameter. It weighs about 16 pounds. Motorists who like to eat their lunch in the tonneau are likely to find this outfit rather convenient.

Another table of unique adjustable nature is the Puffer Hubbard outfit. Except for metal

This table telescopes when carried, as shown in small photo.

An especially sturdy table with a folding shelf.

CAMP FURNISHINGS

fastenings, this is made of wood throughout. It weighs only seven pounds. The legs of this table work upon the principle of a folding lattice gate such as you have seen at the ends of ferry boats. These legs can be extended or contracted as you wish but in either case the size of the top and its height above the ground changes to suit. Thus, when the legs are fairly well contracted you have a table which is 2 feet square and 25 inches high. On the other hand, when the legs are extended you have a table which is twice as

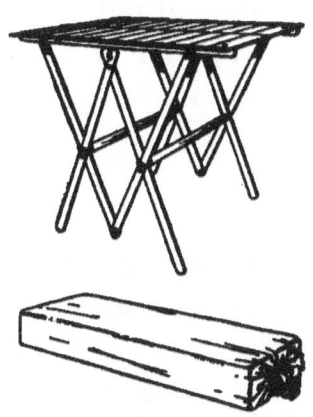

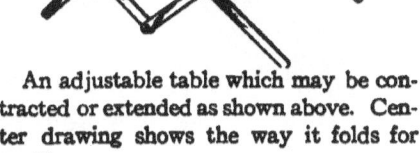

An adjustable table which may be contracted or extended as shown above. Center drawing shows the way it folds for packing.

long as this but lower. In this case, it is 2 feet wide, 4 feet long, and 18 inches high. The lower height is especially convenient when car cushions are placed upon the ground as seats. The whole outfit folds into a package measuring 4 by 6 by 24 inches.

The question of chairs I will not take up very fully. Some of the numerous steel motor-car chairs with which everyone is familiar are comfortable but rather heavy. If you can save eight or ten pounds of weight in a single chair without any serious discomfort, so much the better. If the luxury of a back rest is not considered necessary, the ordinary tripod canvas stool of the fifty cent variety is about as good as anything. There are a number of small collapsible stools having steel frames, such as the Stoll and the Boko outfits, which weigh only about two pounds and are especially sturdy. Of course if one plans to remain for some time in a given camp, a certain number of easy chairs are duly appreciated. One which is exceptionally light and compact for the comfort it gives is the Gold Medal Camp chair. The weight is 6½ pounds and the size when folded, 3 inches by 4 inches by 3 feet long.

A light and comfortable camp chair and the manner in which it folds.

A camp furnishing likely to be overlooked but one which pays for itself many times over is the folding camp cupboard. This is a collapsible canvas box in which are inserted two or three wood shelves. When hung from the limb of a tree or tent pole from above or if supported by crotched stakes from below it automatically expands into a cupboard. You can get one of these from most any outfitter, although they vary somewhat in size and weight. A convenient Abercrombie and Fitch pattern measures 18 by 24 by 9 inches and weighs 3 pounds. When folded, the width and depth remain the same but the 24 inch length shrinks to one inch.

Among other well-nigh indispensable furnishings might be classed a wall pocket and a few clothes hangers. The cook is likely to monopolize most of the room in the folding cupboard but the wall pocket is your very own. It corresponds to the top bureau drawer at home—a place to put things that otherwise would get strewn all around the shop.

The wall pocket is a great convenience in camp.

The wall pocket is a canvas sheet, perhaps 3 feet long and about 30 inches high to which are sewed a series of open pockets. At the top of the sheet are several tapes with which to hang it up. You can probably make a good one yourself.

Camp clothes hangers are quite different from the kind you use at home. They correspond to closet hooks except that you do not drill holes. Usually, they are provided with clamps which fit around the tent pole. One of the best hangers I ever used was a piece of tape about a yard long dangling down the side of the pole. Along the length of the tape ran a series of small hooks. This tape, secured firmly above, supported every piece of clothing in camp.

As regards lights for camp use, it goes without saying that a hand flash light is indispensable. You have your own favorite, and it is as good as any—provided it is one for which battery renewals are easily obtainable. A steady burning lantern of some sort is likewise necessary. At first thought, the brilliant burning gasoline lantern seems the logical light. Some of these are of four and five hundred candle power.

My suggestions concerning lights are likely to sound much behind the times. I must admit that in this matter of lanterns I am somewhat old fashioned. Just one candle power candle lantern or the country store kerosene light suits me well enough. One reason for this is that experience

CAMP FURNISHINGS 159

has taught me that campers do not need a great deal of light at night. They don't sit around and read. They sit around and talk awhile and then go to bed.

For a trouble light or when now and then an intense glare is needed in camp, the spot light provided with an extension cord serves very well. For ordinary camp use, however, I think you will find that a candle lantern answers the purpose perfectly. There is a Dietz candle lantern having somewhat the general appearance of the ordinary kerosene light which is good, but one more suitable for camping is the Stonebridge folding lantern. I have used this outfit for years in all kinds of camping and it never fails to fill the bill.

The body of this candle lantern is 7 inches high and 4¼ inches square. On top is a small peaked roof to which is attached the handle. The sides are mica, bordered with metal. The enclosed candle is so well

A serviceable folding candle lantern.

protected that it would take a mighty stiff wind to affect the flame. The outfit when folded is only about three quarters of an inch thick. So far as candles are concerned, the standard army candles, 2½ inches long and one inch thick, give about the best results. In any case, it is a mistake to use paraffine candles. They melt fast and drip outrageously.

An axe of some kind is needed. All things considered, a small axe with a twenty-inch handle is about the most satisfactory for average going. This does good execution and is easier to carry than a larger tool. The quality of steel, of course, is the important thing; the grade in the ordinary store axe is not much to boast about. The quality of steel in the various Marble tools is above reproach. Whatever axe you take, see that it is enclosed in a sheath. Otherwise it will do damage when you are not looking. For another thing, a camper must be careful where he wields the axe. Cutting green standing timber may often get one into trouble. The wood which a camper burns should as a rule be only dead wood picked up from the ground.

A shovel or spade is necessary. In camp, it is essential for sanitary reasons and while motoring over, sometimes through, dirt roads it is a help in digging the car out of trouble. The telescope shovels similar to those used in the army are very compact and serviceable. A spade with a detach-

CAMP FURNISHINGS 161

able handle is about as good. Either of these is much preferable to a single piece tool.

Absolutely essential in any camp, is a small medicine kit. This may be called upon to do service only in a small way such as a harmless bruise or slight burn, but even so it is worth while. A daub of iodine on such a bruise at the right time may save future trouble. Your medicine kit should include; camphor ice, iodine, cathartic tablets, vaseline, adhesive plaster, absorbent cotton, gauze, gauze bandages, and perhaps three or four additional items.

We now come to personal equipment on a motor camping trip. It is obviously out of the question to give a list of personal belongings which would be thoroughly suitable in all parts of the country. Averaging up conditions and assuming that the motorist will travel through mountainous sections of cold nights and low lying territory of milder nights, the following list is suggested as a one-man outfit which comes fairly close to strict needs with reasonable degree of comfort:

1 suit overalls.
2 pair khaki riding trousers.
3 army shirts (2 wool, 1 cotton).
2 pair shoes (1 light, 1 heavy).
1 pair "sneakers" or mocassins (around camp).

3 pair wool socks.
2 pair thin socks.
2 suits medium weight wool underwear.
2 suits cotton underwear.
2 pair cotton gloves.
1 pair driving gauntlets.
3 bandana handkerchiefs.
3 pocket handkerchiefs.
1 rain coat (slicker, poncho, or raincoat).
1 sweater.
1 light weight khaki coat.
1 Mackinaw or similar heavy coat.
1 pair canvas leggings.
1 cap or felt hat.
1 pair white goggles.
1 pair yellow goggles.
1 good knife (Boy Scout knife is fine).
  compass.
  manicure scissors.
  pocket waterproof match safe (discarded shaving soap tin is one of best in the world).
  needles and thread.
  belt.
  safety pins.
  trench mirror. (Car mirror often used.)
  camera.
  plenty of films and kept in waterproof tins.
  various toilet articles kept in a special kit.

Last but not least, unless your tent is quite mosquito proof, take along a fair sized bundle of mosquito netting. It might also be well to be fortified with a bottle of "fly dope." A mixture of this sort rubbed on the face and hands sometimes keeps the insects away. And sometimes it doesn't.

CHAPTER XIV

GETTING OUT OF TROUBLE

Mudholes—Sand—Pull-outs and Tow Lines—Car Equipment—Tire Chains

It is one thing to drive a motor car over roads with which one is thoroughly familiar but quite another matter to tour out of the way sections where every turn in the road leads to the totally unknown. The latter is usually the lot of the motor camper. If he travels far enough, he may encounter unstable stretches of loose sand, miry mudholes, and precipitous mountain grades each of which will do its best to take the joy out of motoring. It is well to be properly equipped to meet such obstacles if they come.

All things considered, I have found that the average motor camper who ventures to rough and isolated spots has a surprisingly small amount of trouble. Some time ago, while taking a trip through the Northwest I met a number of different camping parties that had motored most of the way

GETTING OUT OF TROUBLE 165

across the continent. In no instance had there been any serious car difficulties. But there had been mudholes—some bad ones. In most cases, friendly farmers had come to the rescue. There was a noticeable lack of "pull-outs" and tow lines in the equipment of these various campers.

There are times and places where mud can be entirely avoided, provided the motorist is in no particular hurry and is content to remain in camp for about five or six hours after a heavy downpour. In many sections of the country, especially in parts of the Middle West, the dirt roads dry very quickly. Considering the mess and trouble which mud represents, the drying out process is usually worth waiting through.

It is not within the province of this book to discuss motor-car operation; and mud and sand might come in such a category. These are difficulties, however, which in the ordinary course of events, the average motorist may seldom be called upon to guard against. So I think I am not overstepping the mark in offering a few suggestions.

In a previous chapter I have classed a small spade as a motor camping necessity. When the car is stuck in the mud with neither a pull-out aboard nor a rescuing farmer or car in sight, one good reason for this may appear. Frank Trego writing in *Motor Age* gives such clear and explicit instructions concerning one way out under such circumstances that I take the liberty of giving his directions. These are as follows:

"If the rear wheels are stuck in the mud, dig holes in front of the front wheels for them to fall into to give the initial start, and if the car does not continue then block the rear wheels instantly and repeat the operation. Place brush in front of the rear wheels and turn them as slowly as possible to keep from churning. If one rear wheel is on good road, try putting on the handbrake fairly tightly to destroy the action of the differential or fasten the mired wheel so it cannot turn and the other wheel will do the work and slide the mired wheel along the ground.

"The instant you realize you are getting stuck in the mud, stop right there and look over the situation instead of fighting the car and burying it deeper and deeper."

Sand is especially mean stuff in which to get stuck. Very loose sand is the worst. Parts of the South along the seacoast are especially endowed with such stretches. As a usual thing, all goes well so long as the car is kept moving. It is fatal to

GETTING OUT OF TROUBLE 167

stop in the middle of a bad stretch of sand for then the rear wheels proceed to bury themselves.

If you are going through sections where there are known sand stretches ahead it is wise to be equipped for trouble. If you have no special outfit with you, stop at a country store and buy a roll of twelve-inch chicken wire. It is mighty mean stuff to handle and carry and I would not have it around without there being a probable need, but it is one of the best possible means for getting out of sand. When stuck, stretch lengths of the wire under front to rear wheel on each side of the car leaving sufficient slack to draw the wire under when power is applied.

The motorist who is up against the situation either of a breakdown and needs a tow to the nearest town or is hopelessly stuck in a mudhole, cannot always depend upon the magical appearance of a fellow motorist or the friendly farmer. The car may come with twenty or forty horse power and the farmer with one or two horse power, but the chances are against either having the necessary tow line. A tow line tucked away under the rear seat of a motor car, like a life line aboard a steamer, is a satisfying thing to have around.

There are a number of powerful little mechanical

devices primarily designed for pulling a car out of the mud, and help in similar difficulties. Most of these can do auxiliary service as a tow line when the need arises. Of outfits of this particular type, perhaps the Pull-U-Out is the one most used. This is a ratchet crank arrangement equipped with forty feet of steel cable, two seven-foot hitch chains, and three stakes. When the car is mired, the stakes with chains attached are planted in the

How the Pull-U-Out type of outfit is anchored out front and attached to the mired car.

ground out front of the car and the tackle between this anchorage and the car is operated by giving the ratchet crank a few turns.

When a tow line is necessary, the hitch chains of the outfit can be coupled together and used for the purpose. There are a number of other ways in which the device does valuable service when emergencies arise. When used as a hoist, it is much easier to operate than an ordinary block and tackle. It may be said that the Pull-U-Out type of outfit covers the emergency field more thoroughly than any other touring device of the sort made. It will pull a mired car out of the mud, tow a disabled one, or right a car that is overturned.

On the other hand, carrying weight may be a consideration. The Pull-U-Out device is compact enough; it fits into a space 4 by 6 by 14 inches, but it weighs 28 pounds—which is very light for the work it performs. The Pull-U-Out comes close to being perfect assurance in getting out of trouble. A fair amount of assurance, however, is possible with a fraction of the weight. The combination of mud hooks, such as are sold by any motor car accessory store, and a length of manila rope may be enough. That is for the camper to decide.

For both tow line and pull-out duty, there is much to be said in favor of a length of stout manila rope about thirty to fifty feet long; or perhaps still more, for a wire rope outfit known as the Baseline Autoline. The latter consists of a twenty-foot length of quarter-inch wire rope having a snaffle hook and manila sling at each end. The outfit coils flat, weighs only four and one half pounds, and may be stowed under the seat cushion.

The main usefulness of the Baseline is as a towing line. One end is attached to the rear axle of the towing car and the other in the same way to the front axle of the damaged car. This line is used so extensively by motorists that a word or two concerning these attachments may be in order.

The wire rope itself must never be looped around the axle or else the chafing and cutting will fray the wire; to say nothing of marring the paint on the car axle. The manila slings are looped around the respective axles and the hooks at the ends of the rope are slipped through these. It is important that the manila slings be looped correctly. If they are twisted or lassoed around the axle, the tow line will stand only a fraction of the strain which is possible when they are properly attached. With everything as it should be, the outfit has been found capable of towing a four thousand pound touring car up a twenty per cent grade.

The Baseline is quite a remarkable little tow line. Yet I do not feel convinced in my own mind that axle attachment is the best towing arrangement. When towing a car with a length of manila rope, one of the best schemes is to tie a sturdy wood bar under and across the frame horns and attach the end of the tow line to the bar at a point halfway between the horns. The

 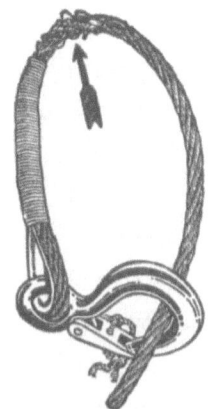 

Never attach a baseline tow line with the sling twisted as above. It will stand only part of the strain of which it is capable.

The arrow points to what is likely to happen when a wire rope tow line is hooked upon itself. Chafing and cutting fray the wire.

The manila sling should never be lassoed in the manner shown above. The tow line will stand only about half the strain it should.

This drawing shows the correct method of attaching the baseline tow line.

Baseline, of course, could be attached to the wood in the same manner, thus relieving any possible axle strain.

An accompanying drawing shows one way in which the Baseline may be used to do pull-out service on the car's own power, provided one of the rear wheels is out of the mud. A length of manila rope can be used in the same general way. With this mired situation facing the motorist, the Baseline is attached as follows.

One of the manila slings is placed around the tire and rim of the rear wheel that is in the mud

Pull-out service with a tow line. The rear hub becomes a capstan.

and the snaffle hook is attached to the sling as when towing. Then, a turn of the wire is made around the hub of the wheel. It is necessary that this winding be from the back of the car, under the hub, and toward the front of the car. Thus, the hub becomes a capstan and the other end of the rope is attached to a fence post, tree,

GETTING OUT OF TROUBLE 173

or telegraph pole, at the side of the road. When the engine is started, the car moves on.

In case the wheels are thoroughly mired, a better way may be that of pulling the ditched machine straight ahead by means of leverage exerted out front. This is accomplished by attaching one end of the Baseline to the front of the car and the other to a stake or post planted firmly in the ground. When manila rope is used, the operations are the same. Halfway between the stake and the car, another stake or fence rail is held upright, a half hitch is taken in the rope, and still another

Another way to get out of mud with a tow line. The central upright stake acts as a fulcrum.

pole is slipped through this, horizontally. The central upright stake acts as a fulcrum and the other pole is twisted slowly around it. The process of winding the rope, together with help from the engine, pulls out the mired car.

As to just what constitutes a complete list so far as car equipment is concerned (apart from camp outfit) is a matter which is mostly up to the individual motorist. Experience has taught him the vagaries of his own car. In any case, this means a full tool kit, complete tire equipment, repair material, and numerous spare parts. You know best. Car equipment will not stand the same sort of elimination as camp equipment. Don't forget extra spark plugs, valve pins, cotter pins, tire tape, assorted nuts, and so on. Also, a piece of stout board about ten inches square will be found a convenience in using the jack. If there are petcocks under the crankcase, these are likely to hit in going over rough roads. It is sometimes wise to remove these and substitute beveled plugs. If not, take along an extra set.

A motometer on the radiator cap is a wise precautionary measure. When your engine is overheating, especially in hilly country, you want to know it. While climbing long grades, the engine will stand especially careful watching. In some of the high altitudes of the West, the power of a motor car is very much reduced. A leaner mixture and sometimes fifty per cent more gasoline is needed than at lower altitudes.

When any amount of driving is done at night through unfamiliar territory, a spot light is a wonderful convenience. There are many legal

First step in attaching chains. Lay chains over wheel with hooks toward rear. Tuck the slack under front part of wheel

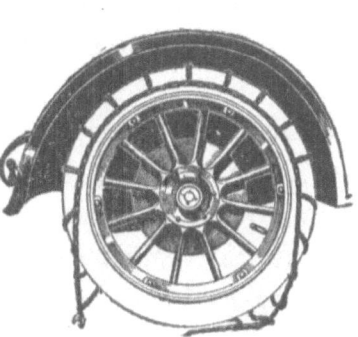

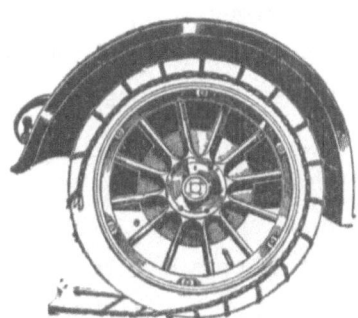

Second step in attaching chains. Start the car forward just enough to run over the slack ends.

Third step. Hook the chains as tightly as possible by hand. Do not anchor them. Chains must be free to creep.

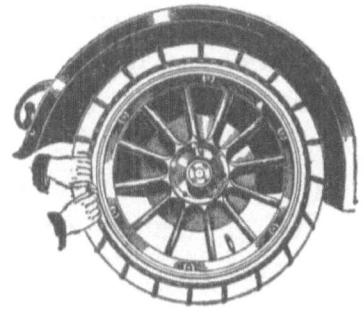

reservations throughout the country concerning the use of spot lights. For definite information upon this score, consult the final chapter of this book.

In addition to a set of tire chains, there should be a half dozen extra cross chains in the kit. While upon the subject, it may not be out of place to suggest that there are few things more warranted to bring a tire to grief than chains which are attached in a haphazard manner. A chain is supposed to shift its position continually on the tire. If held in one place constantly, it would soon wear into the tread. This means that it should have enough play so that it can creep around the tire.

There are several methods of applying chains but the following is the most simple and effective way. Lay the chains over the wheel with hooks toward the rear and tuck the slack under the front part of the wheel. Then, start the car forward just enough to run over the slack ends, after which, hook the chains as tightly as possible by hand. In this way, the chains will have plenty of freedom to creep. Under no conditions should they be anchored.

In regard to the care of the car in general, it may be said that the important thing is to start out upon a trip with the car in top notch condition and keep it that way. This can be accomplished only through careful and frequent inspection, preferably both night and morning.

CHAPTER XV

MOTOR CAMPING TRAILS

*Coast to Coast Highways—Shorter Tours—Guide Books
—Maps*

THIS highway-threaded North American continent is a mighty sizable touring and camping ground. It would be difficult to imagine another land so thoroughly suitable for motor camping. The scenery is unsurpassed in the whole world roads vary but are usually drivable, wherever the camper chooses to pitch his tent he is practically as safe from molestation of any kind as he would be in his own home. He comes and goes as he pleases, with no questions asked.

The long road of the motor camper may have many turnings but it ends only when he himself chooses to make it. There is no scarcity of interesting spots to visit. Any bewilderment on this score is because of the very plenitude of these. Certainly, one could keep continually on the go for a lifetime and not see them all.

The longest road in one stretch leads from coast to coast. Less than ten years ago a transcontinental motor trip was a national event, a daring adventure reported in metropolitan newspapers under flaring headlines. Hardly more than a dozen motorists attempted it in the course of a year. The same trip to-day is of such common occurrence that mention of it has been relegated to the personal column of the home town paper. Twenty thousand is given as a conservative estimate of the number of motorists who cross the continent from the Mississippi River to the Pacific coast each year.

Estimates vary as to how long it should take a motoring party to run from coast to coast with reasonable degree of comfort. One man who has done it says nineteen days. This is driving approximately ten hours a day at the average rate of eighteen miles an hour. The time allotments of others are more liberal, ranging from twenty to thirty days. If one has time to spare, it is certainly a mistake to rush matters. The thirty-day estimate seems the most reasonable if you wish to get the most out of the trip. Of course, many motorists from the East and Middle West drive only as far as the Rocky Mountains and spend the rest of their time camping in the National Parks and Forests. This is often the wisest plan.

There is more than one long road across the continent. There are several. The route taken depends largely upon the sort of country one wishes to see and the time of year. None of the cross-continent highways is perfectly passable the year around. The various northern highways are clear all the way only in summer.

The main traveled southern route is the National Old Trails Road. This runs from Washington to St. Louis and Kansas City and then strikes off into the interesting Southwest with Los Angeles as the terminus. About the best time of the year to take this route is in the fall, leaving the east coast, say, in September or October. During January, February, and March, road conditions are intolerable; they average well the rest of the year.

The Lincoln Highway is probably the most traveled summer route. It runs from New York to Pittsburg, skirts Chicago, takes in Omaha, Cheyenne, Salt Lake City, and Ely, with San Francisco as its terminus. This highway is especially well sign-posted. The motorist can drive most of the way across the continent without once being more than a half mile from the familiar red, white, and blue markers of the Lincoln Highway. The scenery along the way is not so attractive as in the case of some of the other routes but the grades as a whole are easier.

The section of the Lincoln Highway through the high passes of the Sierras near Lake Tahoe is closed about six months of the year by snow. For this reason, it is advisable during spring and fall to branch off at Ely, Nevada, and run southwest over the Midland Trail to Los Angeles.

The Midland Trail runs from New York to both Los Angeles and San Francisco, south of the Lincoln Highway most of the way. The two most northern cross-continent routes are the National Parks Highway and the Yellowstone Trail. These are not strictly transcontinental as the respective terminals of both are Chicago and Seattle. These two highways cross each other and coincide in many places. Side spurs run to Yellowstone, Glacier, and Rainier Parks. They are well signposted, throughout.

Some people who live in sections where hard surfaced roads are abundant in every direction have the impression that cross-continent highways offer equally as comfortable touring conditions. This is far from being the case. West of the Mississippi River, hard surfaced roads are few and far between. The highways are dirt roads for the most part although with occasional stretches of pavements of some sort. In some spots, these roads are very bad and in others very good, largely dependent upon weather. If weather conditions are perfect during a transcontinental drive, it is safe to say that no difficulties will be encountered. One should always be prepared for the worst, however, and the motor camper properly equipped is prepared to meet this. The man who depends solely upon hotels for food and shelter may sometimes find himself in a rather uncomfortable fix.

Of main north to south highways, there is the Pacific Highway on the west coast and the Atlantic on the east. At various points between are several others such as the Dixie, the Jefferson, and the Meridan Highways.

A cross-continent highway need not always be followed to its terminus. Sometimes it is advisable to branch off north or south. For example, one may follow the Lincoln Highway as far as Cheyenne and then branch off northwest on the Yellowstone Highway (not to be confused with Yellowstone Trail) to Yellowstone Park. Presently, connections are made with the northern cross-continent highways and one can either go on to Seattle or turn back east. On the other hand, one may turn south from Cheyenne to Denver, Colorado Springs, and Pueblo, strike the National Old Trails Road at Trinidad, and then continue through the Southwest to Los Angeles.

Detailed information concerning some of the highways I have mentioned can be had by writing to some of the following sources: Lincoln Highway, Lincoln Highway Association, Detroit, Mich.; National Old Trails Road, National Highways Association, New York; Yellowstone Trail, Yellowstone Trail Association, Aberdeen, South Dakota; National Parks Highway, National Parks Highway Association, Spokane, Wash.; Yellowstone Highway, Yellowstone Highway Association, Cody, Wyoming; Midland Trail, Automobile Club of Southern California, Los Angeles.

Anyone who plans to travel for a considerable distance over the Lincoln Highway will find the road guide published by the Lincoln Highway Association a book of great value. This gives a complete log of the cross-continent trip. So long as one sticks to the Lincoln Highway, no other guide is necessary. Especially valuable to the motor camper is the fact that mention is made of suitable camp sites and drinking water in some of the western States.

Of course, the average motor camper does not span the continent. He contents himself with shorter trips through his own and neighboring States. This may mean a tour of the Adirondacks or New England, a fishing trip to Canada, possibly the motor camper skirts the Michigan peninsula, or drives through the fine lake country of Minnesota and Wisconsin. Wherever one goes, whether it be north, south, east, or west, the number of attractive short tours of this sort may be counted almost by the dozen.

For both short and long distance tours, guide books and maps are needed. It is wise to get these all together before the start of a trip. So far as guide books are concerned, I think it hardly necessary to give a full description of the Automobile Blue Books. Most motorists already own a volume or two of this valuable collection of road data. My only objection to these books is that they are cluttered up with hotel advertisements in which I have no interest whatever. However, I forgive them this shortcoming in view of the explicit and reliable way in which they pick out the right road. There are twelve volumes altogether, exclusive of the New York City book, and if a man owned all these he would have detailed running directions for practically every mile that can be reached by motor car in the whole country.

The only means of knowing which particular volume or volumes you need in order to cover a certain territory is either through personal examination of the whole set or by consulting a printed list which gives a synopsis of the contents of each volume. Such a list can be had from the Automobile Blue Book Publishing Company (New York or Chicago). It is advisable to buy only the volumes for which there is definite need.

Another good set of road guides are the T I B Route Books published in Kansas City. These are used to a considerable extent in the Middle West; they cover this section of the country with special thoroughness. The T I B books are published both in national and individual State editions.

Of course, there are road guides and maps galore. In most any city, the Tourist Bureau of Information or Chamber of Commerce will load you down with an armful. This is especially true in the West. A great deal of this free literature is interesting and some of it is really useful. Numerous automobile associations have valuable guides. The Automobile Club of America (New York) publishes a very good tour book which takes in a large part of the northeastern United States.

The maps which come as part of the road book are usually all that are absolutely necessary. At the same time, maps are such interesting things to mull over that one likes to have one or two more along. The long list of maps published by the American Automobile Association (New York) strikes a happy combination of reliability and interest. This is especially true in the case of their strip maps.

This strip map idea is comparatively new. In some respects, these maps are patterned after the Government topographical maps. In each case, a comparatively short stretch of highway is shown, such as New York to Philadelphia, and only the territory immediately along the sides of the highway. In this way, you have a quite clear picture of your route. There is a considerable amount of detail such as cross roads, forks, landmarks, and so on. The actual size of such a map is between two and two and one half feet long and about five or six inches wide. So far, strip maps of only the East and parts of the South are available. In time, other sections of the country will be covered in the same way.

I know of one man who worked out a unique scheme for carrying his map so that he could consult it constantly while driving. He built a map case somewhat after the order of an ordinary picture frame and attached this against the wind shield so that the bottom of the frame was about

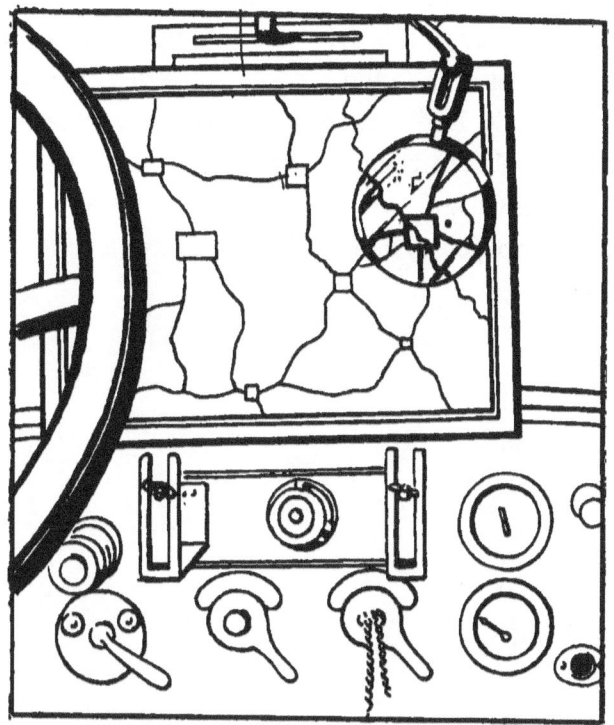

A unique method of carrying a map. It can be consulted constantly while driving.

even with the top of the dash. The inserted map was covered by a celluloid sheet in order to keep out dust. Above the case was a large reading glass that worked on an adjustable swivel joint.

This magnifying glass, swung to a position level with the driver's eyes, permitted him to read his way without moving.

This device seemed to work out very well. As a rule, however, the driver should not be expected to shoulder the added responsibilities of maps, road guides, and sign posts. Whenever possible, someone else in the motoring party should act as official pilot and keep the driver informed. And last but not least, this pilot should have a compass.

CHAPTER XVI

WHERE TO GO MOTOR CAMPING

*Picking a Camp Site—Camping Close to City Streets—
The National Parks—Camping and Motoring
Regulations in the National Parks—The National
Forests*

THE camp-site record of the average motor camper is of interesting and well-nigh infinite variety. One night he may be camped in the yard of the little red schoolhouse, the next in a farmer's orchard, the third on the edge of a mountain lake, and then perhaps the following sundown finds him setting up his tent in the sophisticated grove of a city park.

Proximity to a farmhouse with water, milk, eggs, and fresh vegetables close at hand often makes a suitable camp site for a one-night stand. Before camping in a farmer's pasture it is wise always to ask permission of the owner. He invariably gives this. Of course if on the following day one were to leave a site of this sort littered up with papers or tin cans, the next camping party that came along might not be made so welcome. But I have found that motor campers very seldom do such things.

It is always well to pick the best available camp ground although one need not be so choosey about one-night sites as those of longer duration. It must be remembered, however, that rain pours down even upon one-night camps, so pitch your tent on fairly high ground where natural drainage will carry off the water. Avoid hollow places and, likewise, dense woods. Partly shaded land near the open is the best camping ground.

Very often a suitable site can be found by branching off on a cross dirt road so that you are a hundred yards or so from the main highway. The hour at which the day's drive ends and camping begins varies somewhat with the order of equipment and other circumstances. As a general rule the best plan is to get completely settled in camp before dark and then have an early start next morning. While traveling, it is wise to keep your eye out for a suitable camp site, along toward the middle of the afternoon.

I have said that the night comes when likely as not the motor camper sets up his tent in a city park. This may sound somewhat unusual to

A pleasant one night camp just off a main traveled highway.
Courtesy of *Outing*

WHERE TO GO MOTOR CAMPING 191

Eastern motorists. So far, it is strictly a Western custom. All through the West a great many cities and towns maintain camping grounds for touring motorists. Kansas City, Des Moines, Omaha, Denver, Colorado Springs, and Salt Lake City all have these and farther west they are still more numerous. In Southern California alone, there are more than fifty cities and towns having such camping grounds. They are about as frequent all the way up the Pacific coast. Vancouver, Victoria, Banff, and several other western Canadian cities have them as well.

Very often the section set aside for the motor campers is in a city park. In two or three instances it is the local race track. In all cases, the camper finds a number of accommodations which have been installed for his benefit. These may be electric lights, stoves, water, firewood, toilet facilities, sometimes tables, chairs, and even shower baths. All the camper needs do is set up his tent and make himself at home.

Accommodations vary with different towns but in almost all cases these are entirely free and the camper may remain and enjoy the city's hospitality as long as it pleases him. In some few instances his stay is limited to a day or week as the case may be. This is in order to give the next fellow a chance.

As fairly typical of these hundred and one motor camping parks I might mention Cœur d'Alene in northern Idaho, a city of about twenty thousand population. In a city park, close by a fine bathing beach, is a pleasant grove in which any day of the summer you will find the tents of twenty-five or thirty motor camping parties. Some of these stay only for one night while others remain for a week or more. The surrounding country is one which is prolific in interesting day trips. A camper leaves his tent set up with equipment inside, takes a picnic lunch, and is gone for the day.

It is wholly possible for one to make a fairly extensive tour of the West, stopping each night in one of these numerous motor camping parks. Personally, I would not care to have every sundown find me so close to city streets. City conveniences now and then are very welcome and these city camping grounds perform a valuable service in this respect but there are wilder spots which are more attractive for steady camping.

One never has to travel far to find good camping spots. In the East, there is a wealth of such possibilities in the Adirondacks, White Mountains, Green Mountains, Catskills, Maine woods, Poconos—these are but a few. In the West, the numerous National Parks and National Forests

WHERE TO GO MOTOR CAMPING 193

are the magnets that draw the camper on. Anyone who has the opportunity to visit some of these marvelous natural playgrounds and fails to take advantage of it is missing a great treat.

It is estimated that about three quarters of the motorists who drive West every year include one or more of the National Parks in their itinerary. At any rate, Government records show that more than half the visitors to the various parks drive through in their own cars. These cars come from every State in the Union. And the greater number of these motor tourists carry their own camping outfits.

There are seventeen National Parks on the mainland of the United States. Of the ten main parks, Rocky Mountain Park near Denver is the most accessible—that is, it is the one nearest to the large centers of population in the East and Middle West. Distances between points are greater in the West than in the East but a motoring tour which includes two or three parks in the general vicinity of Rocky Mountain Park may be perfectly feasible. Roughly speaking, Yellowstone is about three hundred miles northwest of Rocky Mountain, and Glacier Park, farther north, is about two hundred and fifty more. There are fairly good road connections. Banff, headquarters of one of the largest Canadian National Parks, is reasonably accessible from Glacier.

The following extracts from a Government bulletin give in a nutshell some of the distinctive features of the ten main American National Parks:

National Parks.	Location.	Area in square miles.	Distinctive characteristics.
Yellowstone	Northwestern Wyoming.	3348	More geysers than in all rest of world together—Boiling springs—Mud volcanoes—Petrified forests—Grand Canyon of the Yellowstone, remarkable for gorgeous coloring—Large lakes—Many large streams and waterfalls—Vast wilderness, greatest wild bird and animal preserve in world—Exceptional trout fishing.
Sequoia	Middle eastern California.	252	The Big Tree National Park—12,000 sequoia trees over 10 feet in diameter, some 25 to 36 feet in diameter—Towering mountain ranges—Startling precipices—Cave of considerable size.
Yosemite	Middle eastern California.	1125	Valley of world-famed beauty—Lofty cliffs—Romantic vistas—Many waterfalls of extraordinary height—3 groves of big trees—High Sierra—Waterwheel falls—Good trout fishing.
General Grant	Middle eastern California.	4	Created to preserve the celebrated General Grant Tree, 35 feet in diameter—6 miles from Sequoia National Park.
Mount Rainier	West central Washington.	324	Largest accessible single peak glacier system—28 glaciers, some of large size—48 square miles of glacier, 50 to 500 feet thick—Wonderful subalpine wild flower fields.
Crater Lake	Southwestern Oregon.	249	Lake of extraordinary blue in crater of extinct volcano—Sides 1000 feet high—Interesting lava formations—Fine fishing.
Mesa Verde	Southwestern Colorado.	77	Most notable and best preserved prehistoric cliff dwellings in United States, if not in the world.

WHERE TO GO MOTOR CAMPING 195

National Parks.	Location.	Area in square miles.	Distinctive characteristics.
Glacier..........	Northwestern Montana.	1534	Rugged mountain region of unsurpassed Alpine character—250 glacier-fed lakes of romantic beauty—60 small glaciers—Precipices thousands of feet deep—Almost sensational scenery of marked individuality—Fine trout fishing.
Rocky Mountain..	North middle Colorado.	397½	Heart of the Rockies—Snowy range, peaks 11,000 to 14,250 feet altitude—Remarkable records of glacial period.
Grand Canyon....	North central Arizona.	958	The greatest example of erosion and the most sublime spectacle in the world.

There are numerous rules and regulations in these parks which it is essential that the motor camper know. The wording of the regulations which especially concern camping is as follows:

Camping.—No camp shall be made along roads except at designated localities. Blankets, clothing, hammocks, or any other article likely to frighten teams shall not be hung near the road.

Many successive parties camp on the same sites during the season; therefore camp grounds shall be thoroughly cleaned before they are abandoned. Tin cans, bottles, cast-off clothing, and all other débris shall be placed in garbage cans or pits provided for the purpose. When camps are made in infrequented localities where pits or cans may not be provided, all refuse shall be burned or hidden where it will not be offensive to the eye.

Campers may use dead or fallen timber only, for fuel.

Fires.—Fires constitute one of the greatest perils to the park; they shall not be kindled near trees, dead wood, moss, dry leaves, forest mold, or other vegetable refuse, but in some open space on rocks or earth. Should camp be made in a locality where no such open space exists or is provided, the dead wood, moss, dry leaves, etc., shall be scraped away to the rock or earth over an area considerably larger than that required for the fire.

Fires shall be lighted only when necessary and when no longer needed shall be completely extinguished, and all embers and bed smothered with earth or water, so that there remains no possibility of reignition.

Especial care shall be taken that no lighted match, cigar, or cigarette is dropped in any grass, twigs, leaves, or tree mold.

Miscellaneous.—Campers and others shall not wash clothing or cooking utensils in the waters of the park, or in any way pollute them; or bathe in any of the streams near the regularly traveled thoroughfares in the park without suitable bathing clothes.

The following are the motor-car regulations in the ten parks mentioned:

Distance apart—Gears and brakes.—Automobiles, while in motion, shall be not less than fifty yards apart, except for purpose of passing, which is permissible only on comparatively level stretches of road or on slight grades. All automobiles, except while shifting gears, shall retain their gears constantly enmeshed. The driver of each automobile will be required to satisfy the ranger issuing the permit that all parts of his machine, particularly the brakes and tires, are in first-class working order and capable of making the trip; and that there is sufficient gasoline in the tank to reach the next place where it may be obtained. The automobile shall carry at least one extra tire.

Speeds.—Speed is limited to 12 miles per hour on grades and when rounding sharp curves. On straight open stretches, when no team is nearer than 200 yards, the speed may be increased to 20 miles per hour.[1]

Horns.—The horn shall be sounded on approaching curves or stretches of road concealed for any considerable distance by slopes, overhanging trees, or other obstacles, and before meeting or passing other automobiles, motorcycles, riding or driving animals, or pedestrians.

Lights.—All automobiles shall be equipped with head and tail

---

[1] In Yellowstone, Yosemite, and Mesa Verde Parks there are some slight variations in speed limits.

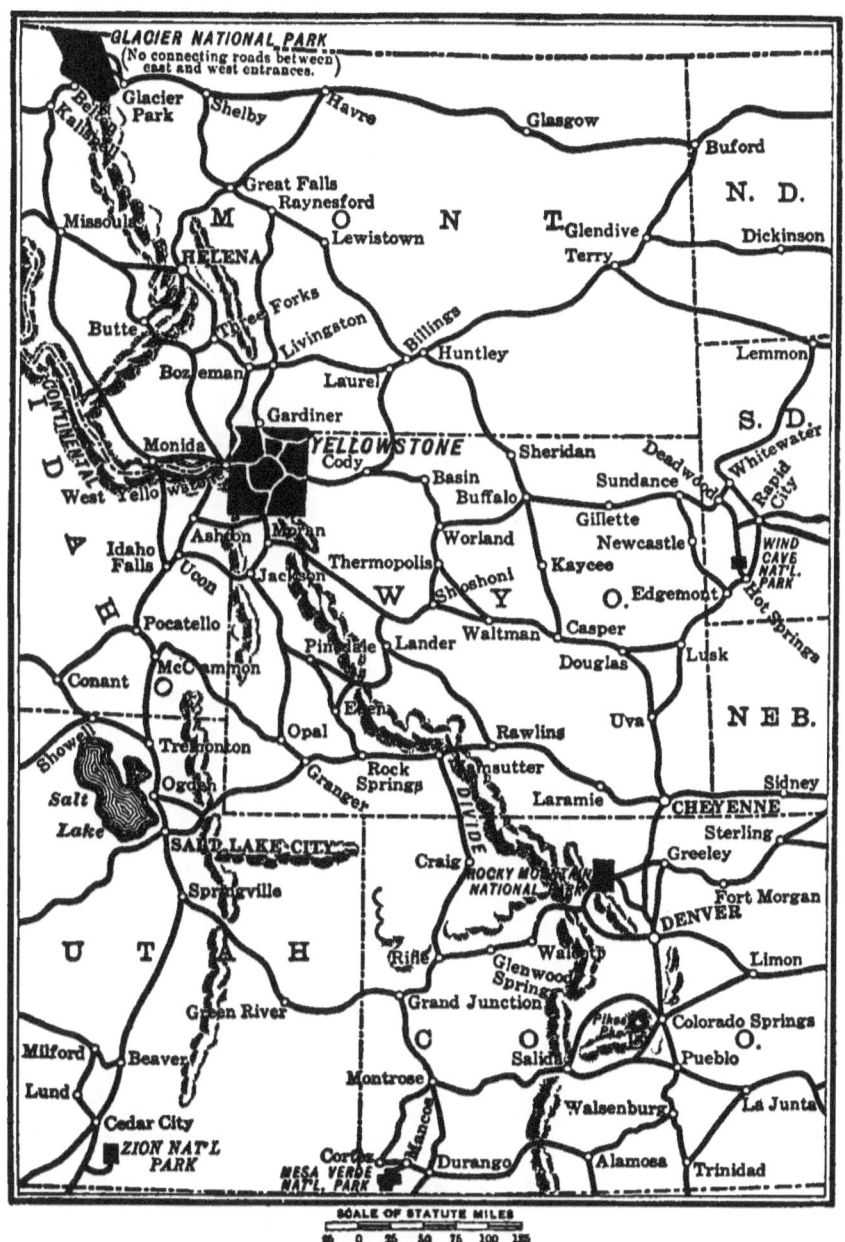

This map shows the location of six National Parks in the general vicinity of the Continental Divide and various connecting motor roads.

WHERE TO GO MOTOR CAMPING 197

lights, the headlights to be of sufficient brilliancy to insure safety in driving at night, and all lights shall be kept lighted after sunset when automobile is on the roads. Headlights shall be dimmed when meeting other automobiles, motorcycles, riding or driving animals, or pedestrians.

Muffler Cut-Outs.—Muffler cut-outs shall be closed while approaching or passing riding horses, horse-drawn vehicles, hotels, camps, or checking stations.

Teams.—When teams, saddle horses, or pack trains approach, automobiles shall take the outer edge of the roadway, regardless of the direction in which they may be going, taking care that sufficient room is left on the inside for the passage of vehicles and animals. Teams have the right of way, and automobiles shall be backed or otherwise handled as may be necessary so as to enable teams to pass with safety. In no case shall automobiles pass animals on the road at a speed greater than eight miles an hour.

Overtaking vehicles.—Any vehicle traveling slowly upon any of the park roads shall, when overtaken by a faster moving motor vehicle and upon suitable signal from such overtaking vehicle, give way to the right, in case of motor-driven vehicles, and to the inside, or bank side of the road in case of horse-drawn vehicles, allowing the overtaking vehicle reasonably free passage, provided the overtaking vehicle does not exceed the speed limits specified for the road in question.

When automobiles, going in opposite directions, meet on a grade the ascending machine has right of way, and the descending machine shall be backed or otherwise handled as may be necessary to enable the ascending machine to pass with safety.

Accidents; Stop-Overs.—If because of accident or stop for any reason, automobiles are unable to keep going they shall be immediately parked off the road, or, where this is impossible, on the outer edge of the road.

Fines and Penalties.—Violation of any of the foregoing regulations will be punishable by revocation of automobile permit, or by immediate ejectment from the park, or by a fine not to exceed five hundred dollars, or six months' imprisonment, or by any combination of these penalties, and be cause for refusal to issue a new automobile permit to the offender without prior sanction in writing from the Director of the National Park Service or the superintendent of the park.

In most of the ten parks mentioned, the car owner is obliged to buy a permit at the entrance. This is good for the entire season. The cost of this permit varies with different parks but as a rule amounts to two dollars and fifty cents. Rules concerning the time and places of entrance also vary. Detailed information on these and other matters concerning the parks can be had by writing to the Director, National Park Service, Washington, D. C. Booklets containing some very good maps can be had free of charge.

The distribution of the National Forests, like that of the parks, is mainly in the West (Colorado and beyond) but they are much more numerous. There are fully one hundred and fifty National Forests on the mainland of the United States and still more are being acquired from time to time. In a number of instances, a forest contains more than one million acres. Such a tract of land, if enclosed in a rectangle, would measure about sixty miles long and forty miles wide—opportunity enough for the motorist who wishes a taste of the wilderness, and as a rule, fair enough roads to take him there.

National Forests are by no means strictly confined to the Far West. If you live in the Middle West or East, there may be one not so very many miles from your own front door. There are two in Minnesota, a number in Arkansas, one in Michigan, two in Florida, a half dozen and more in the Carolina, Tennessee, and Virginia mountains, and one in the White Mountains of New Hampshire. Maps and detailed information concerning many of the National Forests can be had by writing either to the Forest Service, Department of Agriculture, Washington, D. C., or to the Forester of the particular district in which a given forest is located. By consulting an accompanying map of the National Forests given in the present chapter you will note their distribution by districts.

The country is divided into seven Forest Districts. The headquarters of the various District Foresters, to whom inquiries should be addressed, are as follows: District 1, Federal Building, Missoula, Mont.; District 2, New Federal Building, Denver, Col.; District 3, Gas and Electric Building, Albuquerque, New Mexico; District 4, Forest Service Building, Ogden, Utah; District 5, 114 Sansome St., San Francisco, Cal.; District 6, Post Office Building, Portland, Oregon; District 7, Atlantic Building, Washington, D. C.

As regards the difference between a National Park and a National Forest, it may be said that the former always contains world-famed natural features of a somewhat spectacular order. Distinctive characteristics of the parks are mentioned in the synopsis already given in this chapter. The National Forest is also very often a great natural spectacle but primarily it is a huge tract of forest land. Its camping possibilities usually are fully equal to those of the National Park. During the hunting season, its freedom is even greater, for one is allowed to hunt in the forest but not in the park.

Both the Park and Forest Service stretch out a welcoming hand to the motor camper. They more than meet you halfway. After all, they are *your* parks and *your* forests, and there to be used by you. Roads are being steadily improved and in many instances stone fireplaces and other accommodations have been installed in suitable camping sites for your special benefit. The National Park exists solely for recreation and enjoyment; the National Forest is primarily a huge timber farm but a large part of its activities concern recreation. In both services, the officials fully realize that the particular public which they are largely called upon to serve is the motor camper. They are going out of their way to give satisfaction.

The same rule applies in many sections where huge wild areas are administered by the State.

In New York, for example, the State Conservation Commission has recently built along the Adirondack highways a great many stone fireplaces for the special use of motor campers.

CHAPTER XVII

THE LAW AND THE MOTORIST

Non-Resident Hunting and Fishing Licenses—Motor Car Laws in U. S. and Canada—Non-Resident Exemptions—Speed and Light Regulations—Crossing into Canada

THERE is a familiar legal axiom to the effect that ignorance of the law excuses no one. The migratory motor camper will find it most advisable to fortify himself with a working knowledge of what constitutes the law in various States through which he plans to pass. This, the final chapter gives in as condensed form as possible the various motor-car regulations in the United States and Canada as they affect non-resident motorists.

First, however, I will offer one or two suggestions concerning hunting and fishing. It goes without saying that the summer motor camper will take fishing tackle along. Hunting, for the most part, is the privilege of the man who tours during the Fall months. In all States, a non-resident hunting

THE LAW AND THE MOTORIST 203

license is required. The cost varies according to the State. Thus, in New York, the non-resident fee is ten dollars and a half while in Wyoming it is fifty dollars. Fishing licenses are not nearly so steep. Most States require the non-resident to get one but this rarely costs more than two dollars.

A complete summary of the game laws for the United States and Canada can be had free of charge by writing to the Bureau of Biological Survey, Department of Agriculture, Washington, D. C. This bulletin gives all the information one needs to know concerning hunting. In some instances the costs of non-resident fishing licenses are mentioned in this bulletin, but only in a fragmentary way. Copies of fishing laws and complete copies of game laws can be had by writing to various State officials. These are as follows:

UNITED STATES

Alabama: Commissioner of conservation, Montgomery.
Arizona: State game warden, Phœnix.
Arkansas: Secretary, game and fish commission, Little Rock.
California: Executive officer, fish and game commission, Postal Telegraph Building, San Francisco.
Colorado: State game and fish commissioner, Denver.
Connecticut: Secretary, commission of fisheries and game, Hartford.
Delaware: Chief game warden, Dover.

District of Columbia: Superintendent metropolitan police, Washington.
Florida: Secretary of State, Tallahassee.
Georgia: Game and fish commissioner, Atlanta.
Idaho: Fish and game warden, Boisé.
Illinois: Chief game and fish warden, Springfield.
Indiana: Superintendent, division of fisheries and game, State House, Indianapolis.
Iowa: State fish and game warden, Lansing.
Kansas: State fish and game warden, Pratt.
Kentucky: Executive agent, game and fish commission, Frankfort.
Louisiana: Commissioner of conservation, Court Building, New Orleans.
Maine: Commissioner of inland fisheries and game, State House, Augusta.
Maryland: State game warden, 512 Munsey Building, Baltimore.
Massachusetts: Director, division of fisheries and game, State House, Boston.
Michigan: Commissioner game, fish, and forest-fire department, Lansing.
Minnesota: Game and fish commissioner, St. Paul.
Mississippi: Secretary of State, Jackson.
Missouri: Game and fish commissioner, Jefferson City.
Montana: State game warden, Helena.
Nebraska: Chief deputy, game and fish commission, Lincoln.
Nevada: State fish and game warden, Carson City.
New Hampshire: Fish and game commissioner, Sunapee.
New Jersey: Secretary, board of fish and game commissioners, Trenton.
New Mexico: Game and fish warden, Santa Fé.
New York: Secretary of conservation commission, Albany.
North Carolina: Secretary of State, Raleigh.
North Dakota: Secretary, game and fish board, Steele.
Ohio: Chief game warden, board of agriculture, Columbus.
Oklahoma: State game warden, Oklahoma City.
Oregon: State game warden, Portland.
Pennsylvania: Secretary, board of game commissioners, Harrisburg.
Rhode Island: Chairman, commissioners of birds, Providence.

A motor camping party out on a day's fishing trip in the Canadian Rockies. Note the arch of the rod. Immediately after the author snapped this picture, a five-pound lake trout was landed.

THE LAW AND THE MOTORIST

South Carolina: Chief game warden, Columbia.
South Dakota: State game warden, Pierre.
Tennessee: State game and fish warden, Nashville.
Texas: Game, fish, and oyster commissioner, Austin.
Utah: Fish and game commissioner, Salt Lake City.
Vermont: Fish and game commissioner, Montpelier.
Virginia: Commissioner of game and inland fisheries, Richmond.
Washington: Chief game warden and State fish commissioner, Seattle; chief deputy game warden, Yakima.
West Virginia: Forest, game, and fish warden, Elkins.
Wisconsin: Secretary, conservation commission, Madison.
Wyoming: State game warden, Cheyenne.

CANADA

Alberta: Chief game guardian, Edmonton.
British Columbia: Secretary, game conservation board, Vancouver.
Manitoba: Chief game guardian, Winnipeg.
New Brunswick: Chief game and fire warden, Fredericton.
Northwest Territories: Commissioner of parks, Ottawa.
Nova Scotia: Chief game commissioner, Halifax.
Ontario: Superintendent game and fisheries, Toronto.
Quebec: General inspector of fisheries and game, Quebec.
Saskatchewan: Chief game guardian, Regina.

We now come to motor car laws in the United States and Canada. The following summary showing non-resident exemptions and various speed and light regulations are extracts from records compiled by the American Automobile Association and published through courtesy of that organization. These laws are for the year 1920. The immediate changes from year to year are fairly slight.

State	Non-resident	Speed and Lights
ALABAMA	Exempt for period granted by visitor's State—entire year or fraction thereof.	Reasonable and proper, not exceeding 30. Slow down, sound horn at cross roads. No State law covering non-glare lights. When approaching or passing horse or animal which appears badly frightened such person shall cause the motor to cease running so long as shall be reasonably necessary to prevent accident and insure the safety of others. If necessary for the public safety a motor vehicle shall be brought to full stop when approaching a street car which has been stopped for passengers.
ARIZONA	Exempt six months with home State tag. Shall notify sheriff showing they have complied with laws of home State.	Reasonable and proper. Built up sections 10, elsewhere in cities and towns 15, Bridges, curves, etc., 4, outside municipalities 30. Stop for frightened animals. Local ordinances prohibited unless signs are placed. No State law covering non-glare lights or lights on horse-drawn vehicles. Use arm signal when turning.
ARKANSAS	Exempt for period granted by visitor's State—entire year or fraction thereof.	Reasonable and proper. Built-up sections 15; outside municipalities 20. No State law covering non-glare lights on horsedrawn vehicles.
CALIFORNIA	Exempt three months with home tags but must register with Motor Vehicle Dept. 24 hours after operating vehicle in State. No charge for permit. Must have home State card of registration as evidence.	Reasonable and proper; general 30; maximum when road is clear at least 400 ft. ahead, 35. Built up sections 20, business dist. 15. Crossings, curves, 15. R. R. crossings 10. Trucks in excess of 9,000 lb., 25. Excess of 12,000, 15. Excess of 24,000, 10. Headlights of various types may be used if approved by testing agency selected by Supt. of Motor vehicle Dept. Diffusing lenses must not produce dangerous glare. Spot lights must not shine higher than 42 inches. Lights required on horse drawn vehicles. Local ordinances prohibited.
COLORADO	Exempt 90 days with home State tags.	Reasonable and proper, no specified rate. State law requires non-glare lights, also lights on horse-drawn vehicles. City and county ordinances prohibited.
CONNECTICUT	Exempt with home tags. Operators must be over 18 years. Extracts from State law, "Non-resident	Reasonable and proper. If speed on any highway exceeds 30 for ¼ mile or if speed exceed 20 for ¼ through thickly settled districts, such shall be prima facie evidence of reckless driving. If speed of solid tire trucks exceed 15

THE LAW AND THE MOTORIST

State	Non-resident	Speed and Lights
CONNECTICUT (Continued)	shall apply to any resident of another State or county who has no regular place of abode or business in this State for a period longer than 30 days in the calendar year."	on highway or 8 on bridges or intersections, such shall be evidence of reckless driving. Passing of street cars faster than 10 is evidence of recklessness. Mirrors required on commercial vehicles only when view of highway to rear is obstructed. State law requires that spot lights must not shine beyond 30 feet in front and must cast rays to right of center of road. Headlights must be approved by Comm. of Motor Vehicles; non-residents may shade upper half of lens temporarily. No local ordinances permitted to conflict with State law. Stop for frightened animals. All accidents must be reported to Comm. Motor Vehicles within 24 hours.
DELAWARE	Exempt for period granted by visitor's State—entire year or fraction thereof. Special license to foreigners upon recommendation of A. A. A.	Reasonable and proper. Built up sections 15; curves, etc., 7½, in thinly settled section 12; elsewhere 25. State law requires non-glare lights on motor vehicles; must be properly coated, dimmed, or deflected so as not to blind or dazzle.
DISTRICT OF COLUMBIA	Exempt for same period granted by visitor's State, entire year or fraction thereof (except Maryland).	Between intersecting or connecting hwys. 18; cross intersections, around corners or over wooden floor bridges 12. Out of any alley 6. Where not more than 2 houses between intersections 22. Trucks 12 bet. intersections and 8 at crossings. Non-glare lights and lights on horse drawn vehicles required.
FLORIDA	Exempt for period granted by visitors State entire year or fraction thereof.	Reasonable and proper. Maximum 25. Excess of 25 for one-eighth mile prima facie evidence of speed greater than reasonable and proper. Curves, crossings, etc., 10. Passing cars 3. Headlight rays must not shine above 48 inches at 200 ft. in front of car. Dimmers where used must be applied when within 200 feet of approaching vehicle. Spot lights must not shine higher than 48 inches.
GEORGIA	Exempt 30 days with home State tags.	Reasonable and proper, not to exceed 30; curves, bridges, etc., 10. Stop for standing street cars. Lights shall not be reflected higher than 3½ ft. above ground at distance of 75 ft. or shall be equipped with dimmers.
IDAHO	Exempt for period granted by visitor's State—entire year or fraction thereof.	Careful and prudent, not exceeding 30. No State law covering non-glare lights or lights on horse vehicles.

State	Non-resident	Speed and Lights
ILLINOIS	Exempt 6 months if sojourning within state.	Reasonable and proper. Business sections 10, residential 15, elsewhere in cities 20, outside cities 30, curves, etc., 6. No local ordinances permitted. Trucks with gross wt. of 5000 lbs. or less with pneumatic tires must not exceed 25 m. per hr.; solid tires 20 m. per hr.; proportionate reduction in speed according to increase in wt. Headlights must be dim when within 250 feet of approaching vehicle.
INDIANA	Reciprocal. Exempt 60 days with home State tags.	Reasonable and prudent. Built up sections 10; towns and villages, residential sections 15; where view is obstructed 6; outside business districts 20; elsewhere 25. Local ordinances prohibited. Headlight rays must be diffused so as not to dazzle. Spot light must not shine on passing vehicles.
IOWA	Exempt for period granted by visitor's State entire year or fraction thereof.	Careful and prudent. Limit 30 if wt. of vehicle is less than 3 T. equipped with pneumatic tires. 25 with solid tires. 25 if vehicle weight over 3 T. and 20 if solid tired. Proportionate reduction according to wt. In business dist. and towns 15 and 20 m. per hr. on lighting device over 4 c. p., unless designed so that beams shall not rise above 42 in. at 75 ft. in front of car. Spot lights must not shine in face of driver of approaching vehicle.
KANSAS	Exempt 60 days with home State tag.	Reasonable and proper, not over 40. Excess of 40 presumptive evidence in case of accident. Municipalities 12, curves, etc., 8; street intersections 6. Cities may regulate speed. State law requires must not blind or dazzle lights. No State law for lights on horse vehicles. Spot lights must not shine on approaching vehicle.
KENTUCKY	Exempt for period granted by visitor's State—entire year or fraction thereof.	Reasonable and proper not to exceed 25. Built up sections 10; residential 15; curves, etc., 8. Trucks limited to 15. Stop for street cars. No lights required on horse vehicles. Headlights must be arranged so that direct beams shall not rise at greater height than 42 inches at 75 feet in front of car and must give 200 ft. of driving light.
LOUISIANA	Exempt for period granted by visitor's State—entire year or fraction thereof, if home State tag is displayed.	Reasonable and prudent. No State law covering non-glare lights or lights on horse vehicles.

State	Non-resident	Speed and Lights
MAINE	Exempt 30 days with home State tag.	Reasonable and proper. Not over 35 in open country. 15 for municipalities. Where view is obstructed 8. Reduce speed at warning signs. State law requires that no bulb in any headlight shall be greater c.p. than 24. The glass shall be frosted or so arranged that no direct ray shall be higher than 42 inches at 75 feet ahead of vehicle. Spot lights must be turned off when vehicle is in motion and shall not be turned toward any approaching vehicle.
MARYLAND	Exempt for period granted by visitor's State—entire year or fraction thereof —(except District of Columbia).	Reasonable and proper: not to exceed 35, but above 35 is prima facie evidence of unsafe driving. Built up sections 15, outlying sections 20. Reduce for curves. Do not pass cars at crest of hills. Do not pass standing street cars. No headlight shall be so arranged that light shall rise over 42 inches at 75 feet in front of car. Plain glass lenses, also bulbs exceeding 32 c. p., prohibited. Rear lights must illuminate rear license tag for a distance of 75 feet. Spot lights must shine on road 30 ft. or less in front and to right of center. Approved lenses required. Regulations rigidly enforced. Lights required on horse drawn vehicles.
MASSACHUSETTS	Exempt for period granted by visitor's State—entire year or fraction thereof. Where visitor's State does not grant reciprocity then a half fee rate can be had for July, August, and September.	Reasonable and proper; not to exceed 20, outside thickly settled districts. Built up sections 15; curves, etc., 8. State law requires that lights shall be so arranged that no dazzling rays shall be more than 42 inches above ground at 50 ft. or more in front of vehicle. Lights on horse vehicles and sleighs.
MICHIGAN	Exempt for period granted by visitor's State but not to exceed 90 days.	Reasonable and proper, not to exceed 25. Business sections 10; elsewhere in municipalities 15. Reduce for curves, etc. State law requires dimming of lights. No State law covering lights on horse vehicles.
MINNESOTA	Exempt 30 days with home tags.	Reasonable and proper, not to exceed 25. Residential sections 15, congested sections 10; curves, etc., 6. Local regulations prohibited. No State law covering non-glare lights or lights on horse vehicles.

State	Non-resident	Speed and Lights
MISSISSIPPI	Exempt 60 days with home State tags.	Reasonable and proper. Not over 30. Built up sections 15. Passing vehicles or pedestrians, schools, churches, etc., 8. Bridges, curves, etc., 10. No State law covering non-glare lights or lights on horse vehicles.
MISSOURI	Exempt for 60 days with home State tag.	Careful and prudent, not over 25. Excess of 25 evidence of reckless driving. Cities may regulate speed. State law requires non-glare headlights. Headlights must project light so that no portion shall shine above 42 inches. Lights must be diffused and free from brilliant luster. Searchlights must not be used unless light is directed downward or the same as the headlights. No State law covering lights on horse vehicle.
MONTANA	Exempt with home State tag 30 to 90 days.	Reasonable and proper taking into account traffic and condition of vehicle. Cities and towns may regulate speed and traffic within incorporated limits. Headlights must be equipped with some style of non-glare dimmers in order not to confuse drivers of approaching vehicles.
NEBRASKA	Exempt 30 days with home State tags.	Reasonable and proper, not over 25. Municipalities 12; crossings 6; curves, etc., 8. Full stop back of street cars receiving or discharging passengers. State law requires headlights shall not be over 4 c. p. unless the light is arranged so that no portion of beam when measured 75 feet ahead shall rise over 42 inches. Spot lights shall not shine beyond 30 ft. on ground in front of car.
NEVADA	Exempt 30 days with home State tags.	Reasonable and proper. Speed regulated by municipalities must not be less than 12 mi. per hour. Use care in passing horses. State law requires non-glare lights or that gleam not cast over 42 inches above roads, or that dimmers be used so as not to interfere with vision of driver of approaching vehicles.
NEW HAMPSHIRE	Exempt 20 days with home tags. For the months of July, August, and September, half rate. Operators and chauffeurs $1. if holding home	Reasonable and proper under all circumstances. Exceeding 25 on the road, 15 in thickly settled parts, 10 at intersecting ways conclusive evidence of unlawful speed. Reduce to 10 within 100 ft. of R. R. crossing. Electric headlights of over four candle power must be so arranged that no

THE LAW AND THE MOTORIST

State	Non-resident	Speed and Lights
NEW HAMPSHIRE (Continued)	State license; otherwise $2.00 and examination.	portion of the beam when measured 75 feet ahead shall rise over 42 inches. Spot lights shall not extend beyond thirty feet on the ground in front of car. Devices approved by Comm. Lights required on horse drawn vehicles.
NEW JERSEY	Exempt for period of 15 days, if home State grants reciprocity. Same for chauffeur.	Reasonable. Built up districts 12; curves, etc., 8 one-half; country crossings or within 200 feet of horses on highways 15; elsewhere 30. State law requires non-glare lights or that headlights shall not project rays at a greater height than a parallel of 4 one-half feet. Use of spot lights is confined to reading signs and house numbers. Mirrors are required in order to view traffic to rear. Lights required on horse drawn vehicles.
NEW MEXICO	Tourist license must be obtained within 30 days, $3. Issued by authorized garages.	Reasonable and proper. Regulated by city ordinance. No State law covering non-glare lights and lights on horse vehicles. Local ordinances may be made.
NEW YORK	Exempt for period granted by visitor's State—entire year or fraction thereof. May operate in New York City 10 days only without taking out operator's license.	Careful and prudent, not exceeding 30. Cities of first class; N. Y., Buffalo and Rochester, permitted to adopt local speeds. Other municipalities can make minimum speed of 15, but must erect signs. State law requires that front lights shall be so arranged that no portion of light shall rise above 42 inches at 75 feet in front of lamps. Auxiliary lights are subject to this restriction also. Must certify that car is equipped with approved lights before registration is granted.
NORTH CAROLINA	Exempt 60 days if home State grants reciprocity.	Reasonable and proper. Open country 25; residential sections 18; business districts 10; curves, cross roads, etc. 10. State law requires that a lighting device over 4 c. p. shall be arranged so that light shall not rise above 42 inches at 75 feet in front of lamps.
NORTH DAKOTA	Temporarily, if home State tag is displayed. Time construed to be 30 days.	Reasonable and proper. Outside city limits 30. City limits 10; curves, crossings, etc., 7 one-half. State law requires that no light shall be over 4 c.p. unless arranged so that no portion of beam shall rise above 42 inches at 75 feet in front of lamps. Spot lights must not shine beyond 30 ft. on ground in front of car. No law covering lights on horse vehicles.

State	Non-resident	Speed and Lights
OHIO	Exempt for period granted by visitor's State—entire year or fraction thereof. Very lenient in this privilege.	Reasonable and proper. Open country 25. Municipalities 15; built up sections 8. Where danger signs are placed 12. State law requires lights must be dimmed or controlled as to protect eyes of a driver 200 feet ahead whose eyes are 5 feet above road surface. Spot lights must project rays directly on highway at a distance not exceeding 60 ft. in front of vehicle. Horse vehicles should display light.
OKLAHOMA	Exempt for 60 days.	Reasonable and proper. Cities and towns may regulate speed. No state law covering non-glare lights or lights on horse vehicles.
OREGON	Exempt for period granted by visitor's State, entire year or fraction thereof.	Reasonable. Not over 30 m. per hr. Care to be used in passing frightened animal. Front lamps must be visible at 200 feet and headlights must be dimmed or arrange so that rays strike ground not over 75 ft. from front of vehicle. Spot lights must throw rays right and downward. No State law covering lights on horse vehicles.
PENNSYLVANIA	Exempt for period granted by visitor's State—entire year or fraction thereof.	Reasonable and proper. 30 m. per hr. where no signs are erected and 15 where signs are placed. Maximum speed of trucks 20 m. per hr. for less than 7000 lb. wt. Proportionate reduction as wt. increases. Headlights must illuminate roadway for 200 feet and every light more than 4 c.p. shall be deflected so that rays shall not rise more than 42 in. and 75 feet in front. Spot lights must not project rays to left of center of road.
RHODE ISLAND	Exempt 10 days with home State tags.	Reasonable and proper. Built up sections 15. Elsewhere 25. No headlight regulation. State law requires lights on horse vehicles.
SOUTH CAROLINA	Exempt for 30 days provided license of home State is displayed.	Reasonable and proper, not to exceed 20. Curves, etc., 6. Lights shall not be focused beyond 150 ft. and shall be dimmed when approaching another vehicle. Spot lights must not shine on any car in motion. No law covering lights on horse vehicles.
SOUTH DAKOTA	Exempt for period granted by visitor's State, entire year, or fraction thereof.	Careful and prudent, not over 25. State law requires headlight lenses or dimmers which diffuse light so as not to be thrown in eyes of persons approaching.

THE LAW AND THE MOTORIST 213

State	Non-resident	Speed and Lights
SOUTH DAKOTA (Continued)		Spot light shall project rays only on ground. No State law covering lights on horse vehicles.
TENNESSEE	Exempt 30 days. This applies to any State or territory in the United States, Canada, or Mexico.	Twenty miles per hour, liberally construed, according to conditions of traffic. Must stop 10 feet from R. R. crossing. No State law covering non-glare lights.
TEXAS	Exempt 30 days with home tags. After 30 days seal must be obtained from State highway commission. Fee $1 which permits 60 days longer.	Reasonable and proper. 25 miles per hour open country; built up districts 18; business districts of cities under 40,000 pop. 15; over 40,000 pop. 10. When passing others 15. 6 miles before R. R. crossings. State law requires non-glare lights and lights which do not project rays at greater height than 4 feet from road and spot lights must not shine on approaching vehicles.
UTAH	Exempt 30 days with home tags.	Reasonable and safe, reducing for curves, etc. Stop for standing street cars or frightened animals. State law requires that any lighting device over 4 c.p. shall be arranged so that beam when measured 75 ft. ahead shall not rise above 42 inches. Spot lights must shine on ground within 30 ft. ahead.
VERMONT	Exempt for period granted by visitor's State—to the extent of 3 months. Where visitor's state does not grant similar reciprocity then one-fourth fee rate can be had for three months.	Built up sections 10; elsewhere 25. Prima facie evidence of careless or negligent driving sufficient to convict. State law requires non-glare lights or lights which do not reflect beam over 42 in. above road at 75 ft. State law requires lights on horse vehicles. Spot light must not shine over 30 ft. ahead on road.
VIRGINIA	Exempt for same period as home State entire year or fraction.	Municipalities 15; curves and passing other vehicles or in closely built up sections of cities, etc., 10; elsewhere 30. State law requires that no direct beam of light shall shine above 42 inches at 75 ft. in front of car.
WASHINGTON	Exempt 90 days with home State tags.	Reasonable and proper. Built up sections 12; curves, etc., 4; elsewhere 30, slow down for schools. State law requires 2 non-glare headlights of 27 c. p. or less and beams shall not rise above 42 inches at 75 ft. in front. State law requires light on horse vehicles. Spot lights must be directed 6 ft. to right and not over 75 ft. ahead.

State	Non-resident	Speed and Lights
WEST VIRGINIA	Exempt for period granted by visitor's State—entire year or fraction thereof—provided home State grants reciprocity.	Not over 35 miles per hour. Vehicles must be under control at all times. Stop for street cars receiving or discharging passengers. State law requires non-glare lights.
WISCONSIN	Exempt for period granted by visitor's State—entire year or fraction.	Reasonable and proper. Within corporate limits 15; curves, etc., 8; elsewhere 30. Head-lamps must not glare or dazzle. Industrial commission fixes standards.
WYOMING	Exempt 90 days with home State tags.	Reasonable and proper. Not over 25. Municipalities 20. Reduce for curves, bridges, and danger points. Efficient and adequate dimmers required. Spot lights may be used only in emergencies or when rounding curves or turning corners. Local ordinances prohibited.

CANADA

Province	Non-resident	Speed and Lights
NEW BRUNSWICK	Owners exempt 21 days. Chauffeurs must take out license.	Reasonable and proper. Closely built up sections 15; cities and towns 12; where clear view of road cannot be seen for at least 200 yards 20; bridges, curves, descents 6. Care for frightened horses. Lights must be dimmed or equipped with special lenses for non-glare.
NOVA SCOTIA	Exempt 90 days with home tags.	Reasonable and proper. Where view is obstructed, bridges, descents, curves, etc., 15. Open country 25. Cities and towns 15. Lights must not dazzle or blind any other person.
ONTARIO	Passenger cars and drivers exempt 30 days with home tags; subject to special arrange-	Reasonable and proper. Villages and cities 20, open country 25, curves, etc., 10 to 12½. Stop back of street cars receiving or discharging passengers. Movable searchlights prohibited. At

THE LAW AND THE MOTORIST 215

Province	Non-resident	Speed and Lights
ONTARIO (Continued)	ments with each State.[1]	intersections vehicles approaching on right have right of way.
QUEBEC	Exempt for period granted by visitor's State, except taxicabs, etc.	Reasonable and proper. Muncipalities 16; intersections of streets and roads 8; elsewhere 25. Headlights must be dimmed in business sections.
MANITOBA	Exempt 30 days.	Reasonable and proper, with due regard for traffic. Municipalities 15; street intersections, etc., 10. Bridges, curves, etc., 12. In certain rural municipalities 20. Stop for standing street cars. Approved non-glare lights shall be used. No searchlight must be attached to vehicle.
SASKATCHEWAN	Exempt 30 days with home tags. Operator's permit must be displayed on wind shield.	Reasonable and proper so as not to be dangerous to public. Stop for stationary cars. Front lights shall be permanently dimmed so as to prevent any glare.
BRITISH COLUMBIA	Touring permit granted for sixty days free. Automobiles must be registered with Supt. Provincial Police upon entering province. No fee.	Reasonable and proper. Open country 25 miles per hour. Wooded country 15. Municipalities 15. Stop back of street cars receiving or discharging passengers. No searchlight or intermittent flashlight to be carried on automobiles.

Of course, many cities have local ordinances. You can usually get a copy of the traffic regulations from a policeman.

As regards crossing the international border and running into Canada it may be said that there is no formality to speak of. No passports are

[1] The following States have reciprocal arrangements with Ontario: California, Conn., Colorado, Ill., Ind., Iowa, Kansas, Kentucky, Maine, Maryland, Mass., Mich., Minn., Montana, N. J., N. H., N. Y., N. C., N. D., Ohio, Okla., Penn., R. I., Tenn., Tex., Vt., W. V., Wis., Neb., and D. C.

necessary for a citizen of the United States. You are allowed to remain in Canada for thirty days without giving any bond for the return of the car. If you plan to stay for more than thirty days it is necessary to give a bond for twice the estimated duty of the car. You must also deposit twenty-five dollars in cash. The bond must be signed by two residents of Canada acceptable to the customs authorities. However, customs brokers at the port of entry will execute a bond upon payment of five dollars and this is the easiest way. The twenty-five dollar deposit is given back if your car is returned to the United States within six months.

INDEX

A

Air mattress, 82, 100
Alcohol stoves, 60
Aluminum utensils, 50
Axe, 160

B

Baby crib, 29
Beds,
  Bough bed, 95, 101
  Canvas folding cots, 96, 113, 151
  Canvas mat beds, 106, 112, 114, 116, 118, 151
  Car beds, 103
  Combination beds and tents, 110
  Steel beds, 117, 121
  Trailer beds, 141
Bedding,
  Blankets, 91
  Comforters, 93
  Cotton "slabs," 99
  Kapok, 94, 99, 111
  Mattress, 95, 99
  Rug, 93
  Sleeping bags, 91

C

Camp site, 189
Car beds,
  Car cot, 108
  Sawed down back, 104
  Seat cushions and rods, 105
  Suspended canvas mats, 106, 134
Car equipment, 174
Car shelter, 126
Chairs, 150, 156
Charcoal fire, 72
Chicken wire for sand, 167
City camping grounds, 191
Clothes hangers, 158
Clothing, 22, 161
Combination beds and tents,
  As car equipment, 110–123, 134
  As trailer equipment, 137–148
Cooking utensils,
  Aluminum, 50, 83
  Enameled ware, 54
  Frying pans, 50, 53, 56
  Kitchen items, 55
  Luncheon kits, 47
  Mixed cooking sets, 53
  Nesting sets, 48
  Steel ware, 52
  Vacuum bottle, 57

D

Duffle bags, 22, 25, 34, 56
Dust, rain, and mud, 23, 27, 31, 79, 82

INDEX

E

Engine hood,
  As wind shield, 73
  As table, 150
Engine, overheating, 174

F

Folding cupboard, 157
Food containers,
  Combined box and table, 86
  Food bags, 55, 77
  Glass jars, 77
  Meat safe, 55
  Refrigerators, 41, 83
  Running-board boxes, 78, 81
  Tin box, 85
Food supplies, 80, 87
Fundamentals in packing, 20

G

Gasoline container, 43
Gasoline stove, 54, 65, 79, 83
Grates, 70
Guide books, 184

H

Highways, 180–184
  Coast to coast, 179

L

Laws,
  Camp fire, 59
  Fishing and hunting, 202
  National Parks, 195
  Non-resident motor car laws in U. S. and Canada, 206–216

Lights, 158, 174, 206–215
Luggage carriers, 18–34

M

Map case, 187
Maps, 186
Medicine kit, 161
Mudholes, 165, 172

N

National Forests, 198
National Parks, 193

O

Oil container, 43

P

Packing, 20
Personal equipment list, 161
Pull-outs, 168

S

Sand, 166
Shovel, 160
Slip-on covers, 127
Stoves,
  Fluid alcohol, 61
  Gasoline, 65
  Kerosene, 62
  Solid alcohol, 60
  Wood, 75
Suit cases, 21, 33, 48
Suit case covers, 23

T

Tables, 149
Tents,
  Canvas floor, 128
  Lean-to, 125
  Marquee, 131

INDEX

Tents—*Continued*
  Material, 134
  Miner, 132
  Pegs, 136
  Poles, 135
  Tents and beds, 98, 110
  Wall, 122, 130
  Wedge, 122, 131
Time across continent, 179
Tire chains, 175
Tow lines, 167
Trailers,
  Description, 138
  Equipment, 142
  Hitch, 146
  Tires, 140

V

Vacuum bottle, 57

W

Wall pocket, 157
Water,
  Alkaline, 36
  Pollution, 35
Water containers,
  Basins, 45
  Bathtubs, 46
  Buckets, 44
  Canteens, 42
  Milk can, 38
  Water bags, 39
Wood fire equipment,
  Broiler and oven, 73
  Grates, 70
  Reflector baker, 75
  Stoves, 75
  Wind shield, 72

www.ingramcontent.com/pod-product-compliance
Lightning Source LLC
Chambersburg PA
CBHW031059080526
44587CB00011B/739